ENTRU[   ]

A Guide to Intentional Church Facility Stewardship

TIM COOL

ENTRUSTED

TABLE OF CONTENTS

FOREWORD

You've got a big responsibility.

Seriously. God has entrusted His creation and everything in it to us. It's an awesome responsibility. And it's an awesome opportunity.

Have you thought about how this stewardship applies at the local church level? Have you thought of all God has given you for which you and your congregation are responsible? Think about, for example, your church facilities. You likely have a church building or multiple buildings that represent the generosity of many members in the past and present.

What are you doing to be the best steward possible of these facilities? Let me put it another way. What are you doing to be the best steward possible of *God's* facilities? It is indeed an awesome responsibility and an awesome opportunity.

There is one organization on the planet that I trust to guide me and others to be the best possible steward of God's facilities. That organization is Smart Church Solutions.

Let me explain clearly how much confidence I have in Smart Church Solutions. Whenever any church leader asks me for help with a church facility, I defer immediately to this company. I mean it. Anytime. Every time. Allow me to share one of many examples.

I received a call from a pastor in the Cincinnati area. He was dealing with aging church facilities, but he also had a dream for the facilities to be used as an incredible community hub for the numerous residents near the church.

He wanted to know if there was anyone who could lead and guide his church to make the present facilities more efficient while guiding them to the future.

Of course, I had an immediate response: Smart Church Solutions. Over the next several months, Tim Cool and his team worked with this church. I wish you could see the emails the pastor sent me. I wish you could have been a part of the teleconference calls we had. All I did was recommend one company to one church, and Smart Church Solutions made me the hero!

Please read these words closely. We are not entitled to have the church facilities God has given us. But we have been blessed with them. And now, it is our responsibility to steward those facilities to honor God for His gifts to us.

Such is the reason I am so incredibly excited about this book. You have before you the perfect "how-to" guide for church facility stewardship. You have the information now at your fingertips and in front of your eyes. Read it carefully. Read it thoroughly.

But please do more than read it. Act upon it. You have an incredible gift in the church facility God has given you. You also have an incredible gift in this book to guide you on how to be a steward of this God-given facility.

I am so thankful for you who serve the local church. You are on the front lines of ministry.

And I am so thankful for a partner in ministry like Smart Church Solutions to guide you and work with you.

Read this book. Enjoy this book. And, then, act upon the guidance you receive in this book.

Thom Rainer

Founder and CEO, Church Answers

Author of *Anatomy of a Revived Church*

PRAISE FOR ENTRUSTED

Stewardship is managing something that's not yours for a period of time. Through that lens in this book, Tim Cool helps us all see the practical "how to's" to stewarding our facilities well. You'll never walk into your building again without feeling the sense of responsibility connected to what you oversee. Great leaders steward things well!

-Bryan Miles

Co-Founder & Chairman

BELAY

Tim Cool nails it. God has entrusted the church facility to His followers. You might own your church facility, or you might lease space. Your space may need upgrades, or it may be new. Whatever facility you have ultimately belongs to God. You are the steward. Not only does Tim Cool make a great case for facility stewardship, but he also gives you many practical ways to best utilize what God has entrusted to your church.

-Sam Rainer

President

Church Answers

Tim Cool is a leading voice both in facility development and facility stewardship. He clearly understands the gift of buildings and the call to steward them well. Having spent twenty years in the generosity business, I have seen my share of buildings in disrepair while raising funds to enable churches to accomplish years of deferred maintenance. A well-maintained building is not only sound biblical stewardship, but it speaks to the priority of faith and reflects the health of your congregation. When our standard of excellence is raised in building maintenance you can even see an increase in guest engagement and rising levels of generosity. Everyone wants to be a part of a healthy and vibrant church. Well done Tim. Thanks for your contribution to this topic.

-Todd McMichen

Director

LifeWay Generosity

Tim Cool is a tireless champion of facilities management. His expertise and practical guidance help ministries steward their buildings in a way that honors God and promotes long-term sustainability. Tim is passionate about facilities, but more than that, he loves the Church.

-Mark Robison

Chairman and President

Brotherhood Mutual Insurance Company

A church facility is an enormous investment. It can be worth anywhere from a quarter of a million to tens of millions of dollars. Tim brings great help in showing us the value of being good stewards of an enormous resource—our church buildings. Bricks and mortar don't make a church, but they can greatly enhance ministry. Let's all be wise in the use of that huge resource that God and our people have entrusted us with.

-David Fletcher

Founder of XPastor—Expanding the Business Brain and Pastoral Heart

As we navigate what the future of church facilities will look like, stewardship should be at the center of every conversation. Tim Cool's heart to serve ministry leaders is contagious, and I'm thankful for his forward-looking resources for ministry leaders.

-Holly Tate

VP of Business Development

Vanderbloemen

Tim has done a great job of bringing Facility Management to the attention of church leadership in a way that makes it practical, easy to understand, and a necessary part of the church budget. Having known Tim for over ten years, his heart and passion for managing, protecting, and stewarding church facilities is clearly evident.

Tim's ability to provide practical and actionable information to Facility Managers will make their job easier from day one. He has a passion for stewarding the church's largest asset and ensuring good use of the church's contributions for generations to come.

And on a funnier note:

While there isn't an Excel Pivot Table in the entire book, it is a practical and well-written resource for the church Facility Manager, Church Business Administrator, and Senior Pastor to understand what it takes to maintain their facilities.

-Glenn Wood

Pastor of Church Administration

Seacoast Church

Mt Pleasant, SC

There isn't a church or nonprofit leader I know who isn't looking for ways to lower recurring operating expenses so they can fund more ministry. Tim offers leaders both a biblical foundation and a practical framework for facility stewardship. This must-read resource will not only help you manage your facilities well but also maximize your ministry impact.

-Stan Reiff

Partner and Professional Practice Lead

CapinCrouse, LLP

Tim Cool has been passionate about facility stewardship for a long time. Finally, he has put his best thinking into a new book, **Entrusted: A Guide to Intentional Church Facility Stewardship**. Taking care of the physical assets God has provided for our churches is critical. It is good stewardship. We can operate our facilities more efficiently, lowering operating costs and preserving more financial resources for ministry. And, by taking good care of them, we prolong their useful life. Tim has great thoughts on these and many other areas of facility stewardship. If you are responsible for church facilities, you'll want to put this on your "must read" list.

-Jim Sheppard

CEO & Principal

Generis

There are hundreds of ways people find their way to Jesus. I believe the way we care for facilities can either help or hinder the mission of the Church. Tim Cool is an expert in this field, and *Entrusted* will become the manual for church leaders on how to steward well what God has provided.

-Tim Stevens

Executive Pastor

Willow Creek Community Church

Our 50-year-old church had millions of dollars of deferred maintenance we could not afford, utilized only 1 of 7 acres of prime real estate, and averaged 700 people weekly on campus for church and community activities. We felt called to become better stewards of the facilities entrusted to us by God in order more effectively to reach people for Christ and to serve the community. Tim Cool and his team helped us discern an innovative vision from God to rebuild the campus utilizing all the property, adding revenue streams, planning for long-term maintenance, and welcoming over 10,000 people on site weekly. Tim's experience and knowledge are now available to you in this book, which is scalable for congregations of all sizes. I encourage you to take advantage of it!

-Kyle Thompson

Senior Pastor

SouthPark Church

I have known Tim for well over a decade now and there are few I have come in contact with who are as passionate about the local church AND giving us resources to steward the physical assets that allow us to do ministry. You will not regret working through this book if you believe the facility God has entrusted you with is a vital component to do ministry. The book will pay for itself 20x over if you just follow one of his practical steps...just imagine how much money you can redirect if you read the entire book!

-Joshua Blackson

Operations & Ministry Pastor

Elevation Church

Over the years, I've worked with ministries that could have easily prevented some of their facility damage. It takes a lot of time and money away from ministry to fix these things. We have been entrusted to care for God's people and the church facility is integral to that ministry. Tim provides a practical guide that is simple and makes a lot of sense, I found myself wondering, "Why aren't we doing this at my church?" This should be required reading for any facility manager or property committee at a church. Tim Cool is "the guy" when it comes to facility stewardship. We are all so blessed that he's put pen to paper (or maybe fingers to keyboard) and gives us this wonderfully readable book.

-Charlie Cutler

President

ChurchWest Insurance Services

ACKNOWLEDGMENTS

I cannot begin to list all of the people that I would like to thank. That list might be longer than the book itself. From the people that first introduced me to church facility construction, to the leaders that encouraged me to step out and follow my passion, as well as the hundreds and hundreds of church leaders who **entrusted** their facility to my care, leadership, and direction...you ALL are part of this book.

There are some I would like to specifically acknowledge:

Nathan Parr is a facility specialist with Smart Church Solutions and may be the most intelligent Facility Manager I have ever met. Thank you, Nathan, for your knowledge and skills and for sharing them with our team and clients. Your contribution to this book is significant, indeed.

A special shout out to Deborah Ike for her assistance in editing and challenging me through this writing process.

To Lisa, Scotti, Lee, and Jennings...what can I say? I love you all so much and know you all made sacrifices as I traveled around the county to assist churches. Your commitment to me and our family is priceless. Thank you for your support and love.

ONWARD!

INTRODUCTION

Entrusted is not a word we regularly use in our modern vocabulary. Our consumer-centric culture is more likely to use the word "entitled" or the phrase "I deserve…" more often. For those of us in the church, we are likely familiar with the parable of the "Talents" in Matthew 25:14–30. This is by far the most common use of the word *entrusted* to us church folk. As a reminder, let's read this and pick out the word *entrusted* (NIV Version):

¹⁴ "Again, it will be like a man going on a journey, who called his servants and **entrusted** *his wealth to them. ¹⁵ To one he gave five bags of gold, to another two bags, and to another one bag, each according to his ability. Then he went on his journey. ¹⁶ The man who had received five bags of gold went at once and put his money to work and gained five bags more. ¹⁷ So also, the one with two bags of gold gained two more. ¹⁸ But the man who had received one bag went off, dug a hole in the ground and hid his master's money.*

¹⁹ "After a long time the master of those servants returned and settled accounts with them. ²⁰ The man who had received five bags of gold brought the other five. 'Master,' he said, 'you **entrusted** *me with five bags of gold. See, I have gained five more.'*

²¹ "His master replied, 'Well done, good and faithful servant! You have been faithful with a few things; I will put you in charge of many things. Come and share your master's happiness!'

²² "The man with two bags of gold also came. 'Master,' he said, 'you **entrusted** *me with two bags of gold; see, I have gained two more.'*

[23] "His master replied, 'Well done, good and faithful servant! You have been faithful with a few things; I will put you in charge of many things. Come and share your master's happiness!'

[24] "Then the man who had received one bag of gold came. 'Master,' he said, 'I knew that you are a hard man, harvesting where you have not sown and gathering where you have not scattered seed. [25] So I was afraid and went out and hid your gold in the ground. See, here is what belongs to you.'

[26] "His master replied, 'You wicked, lazy servant! So you knew that I harvest where I have not sown and gather where I have not scattered seed? [27] Well then, you should have put my money on deposit with the bankers, so that when I returned I would have received it back with interest.

[28] "'So take the bag of gold from him and give it to the one who has ten bags. [29] For whoever has will be given more, and they will have an abundance. Whoever does not have, even what they have will be taken from them. [30] And throw that worthless servant outside, into the darkness, where there will be weeping and gnashing of teeth.'

OK…the word entrusted is used three times in the NIV. What struck me is that the man who was entrusted with one bag of gold did not refer to the fact that the master had ENTRUSTED the money to him as the first two did. Instead, he immediately went into his backside-covering diatribe. Clearly, he did not understand what entrusted meant.

Staying with the NIV, let's explore some other passages where the word *entrusted* is used (emphasis mine):

1.   **Genesis 39:4** - Joseph found favor in his eyes and became his attendant. Potiphar put him in charge of his household, and he **entrusted** to his care everything he owned.

2.   **Leviticus 6:2** - If anyone sins and is unfaithful to the Lord by deceiving a neighbor about something **entrusted** to them or left in their care or about something stolen, or if they cheat their neighbor.

3.   **I King 15:18** - Asa then took all the silver and gold that was left in the treasuries of the Lord's temple and of his own palace. He **entrusted** it to his officials and sent them to Ben-Hadad son of Tabrimmon, the son of Hezion, the king of Aram, who was ruling in Damascus.

4.   **2 Kings 22:7** - But they need not account for the money **entrusted** to them, because they are honest in their dealings.

5.   **2 Kings 22:9** - Then Shaphan the secretary went to the king and reported to him: "Your officials have paid out the money that was in the temple of the Lord and have **entrusted** it to the workers and supervisors at the temple."

6.   **1 Chronicles 9:26** - But the four principal gatekeepers, who were Levites, were **entrusted** with the responsibility for the rooms and treasuries in the house of God.

7.   **1 Chronicles 9:31** - A Levite named Mattithiah, the firstborn son of Shallum the Korahite, was **entrusted** with the responsibility for baking the offering bread.

8.   **2 Chronicles 34:10** - Then they **entrusted** it to the men appointed to supervise the work on the Lord's temple. These men paid the workers who repaired and restored the temple.

9.   **2 Chronicles 34:17** - They have paid out the money that was in the temple of the Lord and have **entrusted** it to the supervisors and workers.

10.   **Ezra 7:19** - Deliver to the God of Jerusalem all the articles **entrusted** to you for worship in the temple of your God.

11.   **Esther 2:8** - When the king's order and edict had been proclaimed, many young women were brought to the citadel of Susa and put under the

care of Hegai. Esther also was taken to the king's palace and **entrusted** to Hegai, who had charge of the harem.

12. **Esther 6:9** - Then let the robe and horse be **entrusted** to one of the king's most noble princes. Let them robe the man the king delights to honor, and lead him on the horse through the city streets, proclaiming before him, 'This is what is done for the man the king delights to honor!'

13. **Jeremiah 13:20** - Look up and see those who are coming from the north. Where is the flock that was **entrusted** to you, the sheep of which you boasted?

14. **Jeremiah 29:3** - He **entrusted** the letter to Elasah son of Shaphan and to Gemariah son of Hilkiah, whom Zedekiah king of Judah sent to King Nebuchadnezzar in Babylon.

15. **Luke 12:48** - But the one who does not know and does things deserving punishment will be beaten with few blows. From everyone who has been given much, much will be demanded; and from the one who has been **entrusted** with much, much more will be asked.

16. **John 5:22** - Moreover, the Father judges no one, but has **entrusted** all judgment to the Son,

17. **Romans 3:2** - Much in every way! First of all, the Jews have been **entrusted** with the very words of God.

18. **1 Corinthians 4:1** - This, then, is how you ought to regard us: as servants of Christ and as those **entrusted** with the mysteries God has revealed.

19. **Galatians 2:7** - On the contrary, they recognized that I had been **entrusted** with the task of preaching the gospel to the uncircumcised, just as Peter had been to the circumcised.

20. **Galatians 3:19** - Why, then, was the law given at all? It was added because of transgressions until the Seed to whom the promise referred had come. The law was given through angels and **entrusted** to a mediator.

There are more direct and indirect uses of the word and/or intent of the word entrusted (especially as you look at other translations of the Bible and also include the word trust). It is fascinating to see all the things that were *entrusted*:

1. Tasks to preach

2. Gold

3. The law

4. Mysteries of God

5. The words of God; the gospel

6. Letters

7. Flocks

8. Possessions

9. People

10. Etc.

What is the common thread through all of these examples and categories? Someone trusted (thus en-trusted) someone to take care of the item(s). They were not given to someone to squander or to take lightly. They were given intentionally with the full expectation that they would be cared for as if the one entrusting the item(s) was still caring for it.

I have a question: What do we call the person to whom something has been entrusted? Entrustee? Don't think so.

The word is "steward" (as in stewardship...get where I am going?).

A steward is someone who has been given a task to complete by someone else or who has been given something (i.e., entrusted) by someone else to use for the purposes of the <u>owner</u>. **A steward acts as an agent of the owner; they are not the owner!** They are not free to do whatever they like with what is given to them!

Here is one definition of "steward" – "a person who manages another's property or financial affairs; one who administers anything as the agent of another or others."[1]

In essence, a steward is someone who takes care of someone else's STUFF! The stuff entrusted to them. It is that simple.

The key is that when something is entrusted to you, it isn't yours, it belongs to someone else. The one who entrusted it to you has the right to dictate what you do with it. This individual expects you to use the utmost diligence to care for it. You may well be expected to use the entrusted thing for their purposes rather than yours.

The person who has been entrusted (i.e., an employee) cannot merely do whatever she likes, but instead has a job to do, with accountability. If the work is not done, then trust has been violated. If a big task has been entrusted, such as maintaining and managing our ministry facilities, then we should be intentional about how we live our lives to get to the end and hear God say "well done, you have achieved the task entrusted to you." This line of thought has driven me for years as I have served churches and the facilities entrusted to them.

God doesn't entrust tasks…or facilities…to people unless He is committed to making them worthy of that trust! We are to take our responsibility as Facility Stewards seriously. If you believe that everything on Earth belongs to God as I do, then we must accept the fact that our houses of worship, churches, administration buildings, education facilities, recreation complexes, and the rest that we utilize to fulfill the ministry, mission, and vision God has given us…have been ENTRUSTED to us. We will be held responsible by the "owner" of all of these things as to how we stewarded them.

In this book, I hope to convince you that proper stewardship of the facilities God has entrusted to your church is a vital component of ministry and cannot be ignored or pushed aside to deal with later. To help you move forward with your own facility stewardship efforts, I'll share lessons learned and practical tips from my decades of experience in working with churches and other faith-based organizations on their facilities. God has entrusted these facilities to us for ministry. Let's take that responsibility seriously and invest the time, finances, and attention they require.

SECTION 1: THE CASE FOR FACILITY STEWARDSHIP

Before we get into the nitty-gritty details of *how to do* facility stewardship (what you might refer to as Facility Management), let's address what that entails and how it supports ministry.

If you've grown up in church or been involved in it for any period, you've heard the term "stewardship." In almost every case, it probably referenced finances or raising money. Indeed, financial stewardship is a critical element of our spiritual lives, as well as the lives of our ministries.

Allow me to introduce you to a term that might not be so familiar: facility stewardship.

To explain what I mean by this term, let's break it down into its two root words:

Facility / Facilities: "Something designed, built or installed to serve a specific function affording a convenience or service."[1]

Stewardship: "The position and duties of a steward, a person who acts as the surrogate of another or others, especially by managing property, financial affairs, an estate, etc."[2]

Stewardship isn't just about money and finances; it also refers to the care of and oversight for something belonging to someone else. It's very similar to "entrusted." Do you see the similarities?

Even the government uses and embraces the word "stewardship." A section on the website of the Environmental Protection Agency (EPA) defines environmental stewardship as "the responsibility for environmental quality shared by all those whose actions affect the environment."[3]

So, how does this term apply to our church facilities?

Do we believe that God has entrusted our facilities to us, thus making us the stewards of their care and oversight?

I've witnessed churches and ministries spending millions of dollars in the construction and renovation of their facilities — but then fail to maintain (i.e., steward) them. The churches waved the banner of stewardship when raising money to build the facilities, but then neglected their care, management, and maintenance.

To this end, another word that has become germane with this topic is *life cycle*. In general, a life cycle describes the various phases or stages in the life of a product, organization, software, and any built environment, including our church facilities. One component of all life cycles is the "sustain" or "sustainability" element, which merely refers to the ability to last or continue for a long time.

In the case of facilities, when we conduct a regression analysis of a typical facility — factoring in the original cost of construction / development, financing costs (cost of money), and the ongoing operational costs over 40 years — we've found that the costs to sustain that facility equal about 70 percent to 85 percent of the total cost of ownership.

Even so, facility stewardship isn't just for existing facilities; it has its origin at the planning and building facets of a facility initiative.

Intentional facility stewardship starts at the point of dreaming a facility, then planning it and building it. In many instances, the time, energy, and intentionality invested in these "precursor" activities will set the tone — if not the costs — of the long-term life cycle stewardship initiatives. Poorly designed and poorly built facilities generally cost more to operate, thus increasing the life cycle cost.

CHAPTER 1
FIX IT NOW OR FIX IT LATER (BUT AT A HIGHER PRICE)

According to the Merriam-Webster Dictionary, maintenance is defined as the following (as it relates to property, facilities, and equipment): "the upkeep of property or equipment"[1]

Maintenance is what we do to keep our facilities and equipment functioning as intended. It is the process of increasing the utility (i.e., use) of a building by regularly servicing capital assets, major systems, equipment, and areas inside and outside a building. We all do it. If you own ANY property, facility, equipment, or vehicle, you do maintenance.

There are four types of maintenance to consider when developing an intentional Facility Stewardship plan. Some of these are proactive, while others are reactive. Some will save you money, and others are necessary to keep the facility in operation today.

Let's dig in.

Maintenance Type #1: Corrective Maintenance

Corrective Maintenance is probably the most common and most prevalent in any facility maintenance (not necessarily in a Facility Management) plan. It is the "break/fix" work we do daily. It is the "clean up on aisle four" situation. The overflowed commode. The burned-out light bulb and the HVAC system that is not cooling in August. Corrective Maintenance is needed when something fails or is not working as intended. This type of maintenance is inevitable and inescapable. Equipment breaks.

Things wear out. Life Cycles are exceeded (more on this later), and items have reached their reasonable useful life.

While Corrective Maintenance is a daily part of any facility operations, there are ways to mitigate these unexpected time-draining repairs as well as the cost to do so. Corrective maintenance costs you time and money, and in many cases; they arise at the most inopportune times. When our teams are consumed performing corrective maintenance, they do not have the time to be proactive. This kind of reactive method of managing and maintaining a facility is similar to a hamster on a wheel. It never stops. It becomes a vicious cycle.

Maintenance Type #2: Preventive Maintenance

In my opinion, this is an essential type of maintenance your church should perform...NO QUESTION!

Preventive Maintenance is your proactive approach to facility stewardship. It is looking into the future and making intentional plans for addressing maintenance that will extend the life of your equipment and facilities. Preventative maintenance will reduce the potential of downtime and the need for reactive corrective maintenance. This (usually referred to as PM) is maintenance that is regularly performed on a piece of equipment to lessen the likelihood of it failing. It is best to perform maintenance while the equipment is still working so that it does not break down unexpectedly.

This type of maintenance is common for large ticket items like HVAC systems, vehicles (remember the Fram Oil Filter commercial...if you are my age you do), and other equipment that has lots of moving parts. Can you imagine getting a new car and never changing the oil? The oil change is $30-$50...but a seized-up motor can be $4,000 plus...so you can "pay me now or pay me later."

As we have served hundreds of churches, we see that many are using PM's for large items, but not all. And, what is shocking is not even the larger churches with full-scale facility staff are using PM's to the maximum capacity. I assure you that preventive maintenance is FAR less expensive than corrective maintenance. If you want to save money, adding preventive maintenance is one of the best ways to ensure you stay on top of your facility's needs and mitigate a large portion of corrective maintenance.

Maintenance Type #3: Predictive Maintenance

Predictive Maintenance may be foreign as it has not become a household term for most consumer properties and not in the vast majority of churches. We understand corrective maintenance because we all do it...and most of us at least know we should be planning and conducting preventive maintenance. *So, what is this predictive of which you speak?* Glad you asked.

Predictive Maintenance (PdM) uses condition-monitoring equipment to evaluate an asset's performance in real-time. A key element in this process is the Internet of Things (IoT). IoT allows for different assets and systems to connect, work together, and share, analyze, and utilize data. Some examples of using predictive maintenance and predictive maintenance sensors include vibration analysis, oil analysis, thermal imaging, and equipment observation.

Here's a practical example: You could have a sensor inside your HVAC fan housing that could detect fan wobble or some other abnormal operation. Upon detection, the sensor would send a warning to you so you could check on this BEFORE it broke down and before your next scheduled PM.

I believe that as we move more toward incorporating IoT devices in our church facilities, we will see the enormous advantage of PdM.

Maintenance Type #4: Deferred Maintenance

Deferred Maintenance is what I like to refer to as NONE OF THE ABOVE maintenance. Why? Because it is not maintenance at all. It is a term we use to say we did NOT perform the maintenance we should have and, as such, now have items that have not been adequately maintained, cared for, or stewarded.

Wikipedia has a reasonable definition of deferred maintenance. "Deferred maintenance is the practice of postponing maintenance activities such as repairs on both real property and personal property (i.e., machinery) to save costs, meet budget funding levels, or realign available budget dollars. The failure to perform needed repairs could lead to asset deterioration and, ultimately, asset impairment. Generally, a policy of continued deferred maintenance may result in higher costs, asset failure, and in some cases, health and safety implications."[2]

If you are looking at improving your Facility Stewardship and proactive facility maintenance, then do ALL you can to eliminate the fourth type of maintenance listed above and seek ways to be more intentional with #2 and #3.

Unfortunately, over my career in planning and building churches, ministry, and educational facilities, I have witnessed firsthand the use, abuse, and misuse of ministry facilities. I have seen churches spend millions of dollars on new facilities and then neglect to change the HVAC filters, repair leaks, change light bulbs, caulk annually as required, and so on. In my opinion, this is similar to collecting the offering during our worship service,taking 10%-20% out of the offering plate, and setting it on fire. We would all agree that *that* kind of action would be ridiculous and obscene. *"We would never do that ... That is God's money."* Well, who provided the funds to build your facilities? We all know the answer: God provided the resources. It was and is His money. And they are His buildings. Yet, we too often act irresponsibly with these assets.

I find that many church members take better care of their homes, boats, cars, motorcycles, and even their pets than they do their ministry facilities. Is this acceptable to you? It is not to me, and I suggest that the church (big

"C") wake up, take notice, and do something about it. I believe that God holds each of us responsible and accountable for what we do and how we handle every resource entrusted to us.

Growing up in church, I have always heard that our ministry facility is the "house of God." Yet, in many cases, I have found we assume that we can maintain this "house" like you might maintain a residential rental property. However, in reality, ministry facilities are large, complex commercial buildings with sophisticated systems that require regular maintenance. They need not just repairs—but routine, regular, preventive maintenance.

I've conducted a lot of study on this topic. I have been shocked by the statistics and analysis done in the secular markets with facility management services such as hospitals, manufacturing plants, retail, office, and government buildings. Unfortunately, as with many other issues of relevance, the church is trailing the leading edge of thought leaders and forward thinkers by at least 10-15 years, which means that our buildings may be in even more need of maintenance and repair than we know.

The U.S. Navy pioneered a Planned Maintenance System (a system for conducting preventive maintenance) as a means to increase the reliability of its vessels.[3] Since that time, many other industries and real property holding owners have seen the wisdom in Preventive Maintenance.

Here's the reality: When we allocate and expend the necessary resources on preventive maintenance as recommended by the manufacturers and designers, we increase efficiency, reliability, and extend "life" expectancy. Beyond this, there is a significant cost saving when an organization follows a program of preventive maintenance. In my experience, these savings can amount to 15% to almost 20%.

According to a study led by the IFMA, the natural rate of deterioration is roughly 2.5% annually.[4] We have seen this occur at a higher rate for certain building materials and location. Based on our experience, these rates can grow up to 4% and, if not addressed during the year of the natural deterioration, can grow exponentially. Preventive maintenance, like lubrication and filter changes, will generally allow the systems and equipment to run more efficiently and result in even more dollar savings. Preventive maintenance cannot guarantee that you will never experience catastrophic equipment or system failure. However, it will decrease the number of failures, downtime, and distractions of the ministry staff and volunteers.

If you know you have or suspect that you might have deferred maintenance, don't fret. I'll address how to dig yourself out of that deferred maintenance hole later on in the book.

CHAPTER 2

STEWARDSHIP VS. CARELESSNESS

It's important to recognize the visible consequences of neglecting maintenance items (i.e., deferred maintenance), may not always be apparent for several years. Once the signs of deterioration become evident, the repair costs will likely be far higher than the cost of preventive maintenance had it not been deferred in favor of short-term savings.

Let me give you a real-life example. While most people do not realize this, exterior caulking of windows, valleys, step flashing, and the like should be looked at and redone every year or so. A tube of good quality caulk will cost about $2-$3 each. To re-caulk a 20,000- square-foot facility, you might need 10-15 tubes and it might take a person 8-16 hours maximum to perform this work.

If you pay that person $20/hour, the total cost of this work may only be, on the high end, around $365.

I am aware of a church that did not do this kind of preventive maintenance. Within a matter of 10 years, they had to replace most of their windows and sills due to rot. They also had to make other remedial repairs in attic space due to rot and mold. The cost of this **corrective maintenance** exceeded $20,000. If they had performed regular **preventative maintenance**, the costs would have been approximately $3,650 ($365/year times ten years). This represents a difference of $16,350 (more than four times the cost of maintenance) that went to corrective maintenance instead of a ministry initiative. Is that good stewardship?

We think we are good stewards because we are using the financial resources God has blessed us with primarily in ministry-related initiatives (people and programs). However, the example above is a clear representation that *that* line of thinking has robbed the ministry from fulfilling its vision and goal. That amount of money could have paid a portion of another staff person's compensation, paid for a mission trip, paid down existing debt, or provided scholarships to kids going to summer camps ... and the list goes on and on and on. While it may feel like there's a lot of ongoing costs to perform preventive maintenance, performing these functions and duties is good stewardship of the church's facilities and allows the church to fulfill its mission. Thus, it is better to spend "dimes vs. dollars."

Let me give you another example that will look at both the savings of preventive maintenance and also operational cost savings—the ever-desirable double whammy. This example will be exploring one of the most expensive systems in your building, and one that can save you the highest amount in life cycle cost and operational savings: the heating, ventilation and air conditioning (HVAC) system.

"I haven't spent any money on preventive maintenance for over two years" was a quote shared with me from an HVAC service company about a building owner. The building owner was very proud of this fact and was bragging about it. So, the service representative asked if they could tour the roof to do a cursory inspection of the units. Upon arriving on the roof and opening up the service door of the 10-ton unit, they discovered that the filter had never been changed and was so filthy that it looked like a "shag rug." After removing the filter (if you can call it that after it had been transformed into a shag rug), the service representative found a thick layer of filth on the coil. With these two layers of crud and filth, there was virtually no air flowing through the unit. To give you a sense of what this means, consider that you are getting ready to drive your car on a 90-degree day, and you place cardboard over your radiator. What do you think would happen to your engine? RIGHT, it would overheat. The same thing applies to your HVAC unit. In this case, they replaced the filter and cleaned the coils, but the unit was so badly worn that it still failed one month later. In this case, the service representative told me that the cost of the preventive maintenance would have been $500-750 per year or $1,000-$1,500 for the two-years. Instead, the owner paid about $15,000 to replace a two-year-old unit.

This does not seem like excellent stewardship, and he was not bragging anymore.

CHAPTER 3

THE REAL COST OF OWNERSHIP

While we're on the topic of finances, let's address the real cost of owning a facility. One trend I've noticed as I've served over 1000 churches is a lack of understanding among ministry leaders regarding the full cost of facility ownership (not just the cost to build). It's understandable to think that once you've gone through the arduous process of buying or building a facility, that the most significant costs are known and accounted for. However, the truth is that the ongoing expenses eclipse the initial costs and in a shorter period than most would imagine.

Let's look at the REAL cost of ownership of our ministry facility. The following is a theoretical example of the cost of owning a ministry facility.

Initial Cost:

For this exercise, let's assume our new ministry facility is 30,000 square feet. We can have it built for $180/square foot (this is going to be low for some parts of the country and does not include site work, AVL, furnishings, etc.), and we paid the design professional a fee of 7% of the construction value. We will also assume the land has been paid for and is unencumbered by debt.

So what do the numbers look like?

INITIAL COST: 30,000 square feet x $180/square feet = $5,400,000 plus the cost mentioned above.

Cost of "Money":

Let's assume we borrowed $4,000,000 to pay for the project and did so based on a 15-year loan at 4.5% but paid it off in seven years. In this scenario, you will have paid approximately $1.0M in interest.

Cost of Operation:

Based on our research, the average church in America will spend $6.00 to $7.00 per square foot annually for janitorial services, utilities and general maintenance, including staffing.

In addition, a church will spend roughly $1.00 (only use if it is a brand-new building) to $3.00 per square foot in capital improvements if the capital reserve account is started at the time construction is complete. (This number grows significantly higher if you neglect the capital reserve account during the early years of the building's life cycle).

For the sake of this exercise, let's assume we will spend $6.50/square foot for operations and $1.00/square foot for capital reserve items (only because this is a new building...otherwise it would need to be higher). This may be low, but I want the calculations to be realistic.

30,000 square feet x $7.50/square foot = $225,000/year

Assume a 40 year life cycle (which is not that long) at 1.5% per year of inflation. Remember, that operational costs are perpetual and paid for with inflated dollars so this is going to increase, and 1.5% is probably too low.

$225,000/year x 40 years = $9,000,000 + 60% (1.5% per year inflation for 40 years without compounding) = $14,400,000

So let's look at what this means:

- Initial costs including design - $5,400,000
- Cost of Money - $1,000,000
- Cost of life cycle operations and capital reserve - $14,400,000 (that is $480/square foot...OUCH)
- TOTAL COST OF OWNERSHIP = $20,800,000

WOW! That is a BIG number, here is the shocking part:

- The combined cost of the construction partner and the design professionals is only 3% of the total cost of ownership.
- The construction cost, including the design, is only about 23% of the total cost of ownership.
- The interest paid is only about 5-6% of the total cost of ownership.
- Leaving at least 71% of the total cost of ownership in operation costs and capital expenditures.

In his book, Life Cycle Cost Analysis 2: Using it in Practice, David S. Haviland states:

"The initial design and construction of a facility comprises about 15% of the total cost of a building over its 40 year lifespan. The remaining 85% is made up of the building's operations and maintenance costs."[1]

So what costs more, the initial cost, or the cost after you occupy? I think the numbers speak for themselves. Do we invest the same amount of time and energy in planning our operational costs as we did when we developed our physical master plans and floor plans? Why do we get upset about an architect charging 8% instead of 5%, or the construction partner charging 9% instead of 4%? The fees that encompass only 3% of the total cost of ownership feel so important at the time we hire these professionals.

The decisions, direction, means, and methods this team suggests and implements will be with you for the life of your buildings. Do we have our eyes on the REAL cost of facility ownership?

If Facility Stewardship is really about being wise stewards of all God has entrusted to us, then I think it is fair to say most of us have our priorities upside down. Facility Stewardship must include proactive facility management and long-term care. This is where we too often fall grossly short in our Facility Stewardship initiative.

CHAPTER 4

ENERGY SAVINGS EQUALS GOOD STEWARDSHIP

O ne way you can reduce your total cost of ownership is by leveraging energy savings opportunities. In addition to the extended life of the HVAC unit, (generally, you can obtain a 20% longer useful life by implementing regular maintenance, which means you have reduced your "ownership cost") there are significant energy savings. If your facility is completely powered by electricity, your HVAC load as a percentage of the total utility cost is usually 50%-75%.

According to the American Society of Heating, Refrigerating, and Air Conditioning Engineers (www.ashrae.org), if you do not provide regular cleaning of your condensing coils (the coils on the exterior units), you will increase your energy consumption by as much as 30%[1]. Also, if you do not routinely clean the evaporator coil (the coil on the inside units), you will consume additional energy. That is a ton (quite literally) of power.

Let us look at how much. If you have a 20,000-square-foot facility and your average annual electric bills are $1.50/square foot, you would have bills totaling $30,000. If we take 60% of that as being the HVAC load, we could allocate $18,000 for the HVAC consumption. If we then look at what the added cost could be for poor maintenance practice and reduce the 55% from above (36% + 19%) to 30%, that would be an added utility cost of $5,400 per year in energy costs. That does not take into account the strong likelihood that this drain on the system will also reduce the useful life of the units and increase repairs and service calls.

If the filters had been changed and the coils cleaned two times a year (which is the minimum), you would have costs of about $1,000 a year, which still nets a savings of about $4,400 per year that is directly available for ministry initiative—which is the core purpose for the existence of the church.

CHAPTER 5

FIRST IMPRESSIONS...ONLY ONE SHOT

What we have discussed so far is important. Being wise stewards of the resources entrusted to us is paramount. However, I want to challenge you to remember that first, nothing we do is ever merely about us and, second, everything we do or do not do has eternal consequences. Whether you like it or not, first impressions are essential. Studies have shown that people often make up their minds to attend or return to a church based on what they see. How we steward our facilities will have an impact on your guests. Period.

One spring, I was driving with the family after church to meet friends for an Easter afternoon lunch. We passed a church that had an Easter message on their roadside sign with attached balloons to draw attention to the sign. But the weeds were so high you could barely read the sign, and they had not cleaned up the parking lot in months.

The message of their sign was incongruent with the appearance of their property.

Over time, "deferred maintenance" begins to leave its mark. What do you think your guests think when they enter your parking lot, walk toward the building, and step inside the facility? Will the "house of God" be an appealing place?

Will guests want to return? Will they be confident that their children will be in a safe, clean space? For those of us who attend church regularly, because we are grounded in our faith and in the ministries we serve, we tend to overlook the visible issues. However, what about the first-time guest who may be making a church-home decision? Do you think they will notice the duct tape patching the carpet in the foyer? Will they notice the odor in our restrooms and nursery area? Will they see the cracks in our parking lot and sidewalks or the pond that forms on rainy days? When was the last time you walked through your facility with a guest's perspective?

In his book "First Impressions," Mark Waltz, former Pastor of Connection at Granger Community Church in Granger, Ind., addresses what it may be like to be a guest in our churches and how the first impression may not always be the best. After all, the first impression may be the only chance we have to impact their lives. He writes, "When your guests are distracted from the real purpose of their visit to your church, you'll have a difficult time re-engaging them. In order for people to see Jesus, potential distractions must be identified and eliminated."[1]

Have you ever considered that the condition of your buildings could affect your ability to engage and minister to people? You may be thinking, *"The gospel is compelling enough, the buildings are only a tool and we need to focus more on delivering the gospel message than on worrying about our buildings."* Whether we like to admit it or not, first-time guests will consider all elements of their experience at your church, including the facilities, and will judge you by all of the elements of their experience. I am not suggesting this is right, and I am definitely not saying that the gospel is not compelling. But to close a blind eye to the overall experience and impact of your facilities is just foolish. We live in a consumer-minded world, whether we like it or not, and many—if not all—of your guests will determine their experiences from all of these elements.

So, if saved money does not get your attention to implement a Facility Stewardship initiative, then the furtherance of the gospel should. Although the investment might appear high, it will generate significant cost savings in the long run, which in turn frees up funds to be used for ministry.

Now that is exciting to me. With that in mind, let's dive into the day-to-day operations of stewarding your church facilities

Section 2: Operations - The Nuts & Bolts of Facility Stewardship

Hopefully, by now, I've convinced you that properly caring for your church's facilities is a crucial aspect of ministry. When done with excellence, you will not only help guests feel welcomed, but you will save the church money and extend the life of your facility and equipment. How that all happens is what we'll address next.

Here is where we will get really practical. After all, buildings don't clean themselves, nor does equipment perform self-maintenance (Don't we wish!). With that in mind, let's address the details of what it takes to steward your facilities properly.

On a regular basis, there are tasks we must complete to care for and maintain a facility such as:

- Vacuum
- Dust
- Inspect fire extinguishers
- Test emergency exit lights

- Confirm first aid supplies are up-to-date and fully stocked
- Clean and restock restrooms
- Replace lightbulbs
- Review Safety Data Sheets
- Schedule maintenance for the HVAC system
- Check and clean gutters
- Refresh landscaping
- Repair potholes in the parking lot
- Check flooring for stains or other damage
- Re-caulk window sills
- Ensure no electrical outlet is overloaded
- …and much more…

Often, the person (or team, hopefully) responsible for facility maintenance also handles setup and teardown of rooms for services and special events plus a whole host of "additional duties as required." (You know, that ambiguous line conveniently placed at the end of every job description.) With all that's entailed in facility stewardship, it's essential to be intentional and develop a plan to make it work. Sound overwhelming? No need to throw your hands up in despair. In the following chapters, I'll cover the details of how to get started with your maintenance program, save on utilities, keep up with janitorial tasks, and much more.

CHAPTER 6

THE ART OF PREVENTATIVE MAINTENANCE

The best way to save money, prevent emergencies (because no one wants the heat to go out in a New York winter), and keep your church facilities running well is through a preventative maintenance plan. The art of preventive maintenance involves noticing small problems and fixing them before significant problems develop. A structural or mechanical breakdown is usually preceded by a long period of deterioration, which people tend to neglect because it is not obvious. A piece of equipment that is not lubricated on schedule, for example, will continue to function until a bearing burns out. Similarly, eroded mortar joints may be overlooked until a brick wall buckles. Preventive maintenance does not necessarily require a high degree of technical skill on the part of the Facility Manager. It is essential, however, that the manager understands what services are needed and arranges for competent service.

The following is a preliminary checklist of items that every church should consider as a minimum baseline for maintaining their facility.

- Custodial - Regular schedule for cleaning all areas of the facility (inside and outside)
- HVAC - Changing filters, preventative maintenance, etc.
- Electrical - Compliance with electrical codes, childproofed outlets where appropriate
- Water heaters - Inspected and drained as appropriate
- Kitchens - Inspect vent hoods, check for expired food items
- Painting - Schedule for paint touch-ups or full repainting

- Landscaping - Regular schedule for grounds upkeep, maintaining outdoor signage, inspect playground equipment
- Parking lot - Painting stripes, fixing cracks or potholes
- Lighting - Check emergency and exit lighting, replace bulbs, etc.
- Flooring - Cleaning, repairing, and replacing as needed
- Roof - Inspect the roof annually and after potential damage (storms, hail, etc.)
- Baptistery - Drain and test
- Smoke and Carbon monoxide detectors - Inspect and replace batteries
- Drinking fountains - Address functional issues such as chemical buildup
- Restrooms - Schedule for keeping bathrooms stocked, cleaned, and functioning

For a detailed checklist, go to:

http://www.smartchurchsolutions.com/entrustedresources.

CHAPTER 7

DEFERRED MAINTENANCE (AKA...WHAT WE PUT OFF FOR LATER...)

H ere's where we pause to address the elephant in the room… *"Yes, I know we should do preventative maintenance, but we haven't been consistent. How do we handle that situation?"*

What you have here is called "deferred maintenance."

Let's explore the keys to conquering deferred maintenance.

Key #1: Identify YOUR deferred maintenance

The first step in nearly any issue in life is first to recognize the fact that there is indeed an issue. If we do not acknowledge there is an issue, how can we resolve it? Most churches have a lack of understanding when it comes to their deferred maintenance problem. We get so busy with budgets, "doing church", break/fix items, etc. that we do not take the time to see the trees for the forest. Even those who take the time may not know what to look for. This situation is where a set of "fresh eyes" can be beneficial. You can hire a professional to come in and evaluate your church facilities for you (hint…we offer this service at Smart Church Solutions). Or you could ask someone not affiliated with your church to walk the facilities and tell you what they observe. This effort will give you a list of items that need attention (i.e., your deferred maintenance).

Key #2: Provide adequate general maintenance budgets

Over the last several years, we have done facility assessments for several million square feet of church facilities. The aggregate amount of deferred maintenance has been in the tens of millions of dollars. That is sad! The church, as a whole, claims to be an organization focused on being good stewards, and yet we allow our buildings to deteriorate right under our feet.

In every single case, the General Maintenance budget was under-funded. There was not enough money in the budget to keep up with the natural rate of physical deterioration. Check out this quote from Kevin Folsom, former Facilities Director at Dallas Theological Seminary:

"There are numerous levels that can be used to go about this, but to start we have to remember our early Physics lessons in high school about the 2nd Law of Thermodynamics. Everything we build will decay, but it may last longer if properly maintained. So, here's a puzzling question…If we build facilities that the natural law causes them to decay at fairly predictable rates throughout its birth to burial, why do we not plan for it?"[1]

The best way to conquer deferred maintenance is to have a budget that addresses the natural decay and deterioration of your facility.

Key #3: Properly staff your facility team

In every instance referenced above, not only were the budgets under-funded, but the facility teams were severely understaffed! If you only have enough staff to address the break/fix emergencies of the urgent, how do you expect to stay on top of the natural decay and deterioration? Quick answer - YOU CAN'T! Based on national surveys by our firm and IFMA, we believe the number of facility staff for a well-run organization is one Full Time Facility Staff Employee for every 25,000 – 35,000 SF. This is not for cleaning (that's another story), but only for general maintenance.

Key #4: Have a well funded Capital Reserve Plan

Church leader...capital replacement is not an "IF" consideration but rather a "WHEN" and "HOW MUCH." You WILL replace every HVAC unit. You WILL replace all your carpet. You WILL replace your roof. You WILL have to resurface your parking lot. To turn a blind eye to the need of a capital reserve fund is kin to telling God that the laws of science and natural resources...that HE created...don't apply to your church. Somehow I doubt that's what you intend to communicate. After all, you probably have a 401(k) or similar account for your retirement.

If we were proactive with our operational budgets and capital reserves, there would not be any deferred maintenance. In a perfect world, we would properly fund our general maintenance budget to keep the building in the best physical condition possible...AND...we would have adequate capital reserves when we approach the "end of life" of any facility component.

That is how you conquer deferred maintenance. There's nothing easy or quick about digging out of a deferred maintenance hole. However, it is vital that you invest the time and money to do so. I'll address budgets in a subsequent chapter since I realize this often comes down to *"We'd like to, but we don't have the money."*

CHAPTER 8

UTILITIES: KEEPING THE LIGHTS ON...BUT NOT ALL THE TIME

Once you have a good handle on preventative maintenance and have caught up on deferred maintenance, another item to review is the church's utilities. This is an area where you might be spending more money than is necessary. In late 2019, Smart Church Solutions performed a Church Facility Operations Benchmarking Assessment to evaluate how churches of comparable size and operational tempos perform. (You can download the full report at http://www.smartchurchsolutions.com/entrustedresources). One aspect of this assessment was to gather information regarding utility costs. In our survey, respondents spent $1.38 per square foot on utilities (gas and electric combined).

What if our utility costs are too high?

The largest area of operational savings is tied to utility costs; at least it is the most visible since we get a utility bill each month. For most of us, this is an OUCH each month. On average, a church's utility bill will consume $1.00 to $1.50/square foot annually. On a 100,000 square foot facility, that is $100,000 to $150,000 over the course of a year. That is REAL money. The cost of keeping the lights on could pay the salary of several staff members.

What if we could reduce our energy consumption by 10%, 20%, or more? What other ministry initiatives could we start or enlarge? What could we invest in a capital reserve account? How many of my three kids could you have sent to college for me? (Just wanted to see if you were still with me.)

Here are several practical, and yet simple, ways to reduce utility costs:

Tip #1: Reduce Your HVAC Power Consumption

For most churches, the consumption of energy to heat and cool their facilities equates to 50-75% of their utility bill. The greatest opportunity to have a significant impact on your costs is by exploring energy savings with these systems.

Here are some suggestions:

Change Your Set Points

This may sound overly simplistic, but it is still one of the best and least expensive means to reduce energy consumption. Whether you are using a manual thermostat or a full-blown Building Automation System, for each degree you lower your thermostat (for heat); you will reduce your utility bill by an average of 1%. In cooling mode, each degree you set your thermostat above 75 degrees Fahrenheit cuts your cooling costs by 3%. If we continue with our example above, assuming you are spending $1.25/square foot or $125,000 annually and that 60% of your utility bills are for heating and cooling ($75,000) and that you change your set points by two degrees, you could save about $1,500 annually.

Use Programmable Thermostats

For some of you, this is going to sound elementary, but I assure you there are far more churches using manual thermostats than you realize...really! According to Energy Star (www.energystar.gov), you can save about 8% a year by properly setting a programmable thermostat (vs. a manual thermostat) and maintaining those settings.[1]

Move Toward Building Automation

Now, don't let this overwhelm you, but there are several different levels of complexity associated with the generic term "building automation system" (BAS). According to the EPA's "Greening EPA Glossary," a BAS can be defined as, "A system that optimizes the start-up and performance of HVAC equipment (and alarm systems). A BAS greatly increases the interaction between the mechanical subsystems of a building, improves occupant comfort, lowers energy use, and allows off-site building control."[2]

Type #1: BAS/IBS

You will also hear this referred to as a "Building Management System" and even "Intelligent Building Systems." In layman's terms, it is any type of system that helps you control building systems operations, primarily HVAC systems. They are generally a computer-based control system installed in buildings to control and monitor the building's mechanical and electrical equipment such as ventilation, lighting, power systems, fire systems, and security systems. A BAS usually consists of software and hardware and has many forms and price points.

Type #2: PC/Computer-Based Systems

In these systems, there is a system controller that is generally run by a laptop or other type of computer. There is proprietary software that runs on the computer and interfaces with the actual system hardware to set schedules, monitor system challenges, track system issues, and many other functions.

Type #3: Interface HVAC System with Room Scheduling Software

A couple of the independent room scheduling software programs available to the church market now offer some interface with HVAC systems. In the case of our system, eSPACE:

(https://www.smartchurchsolutions.com/integrations/hvac), a church can subscribe to the interface and the system can communicate with a BAS, a 'stand-alone' communicating thermostat solution (like COOLSPACE), or with freestanding wireless/WiFi thermostats. These interface programs allow you to engage and disengage your HVAC systems based on the actual room usage and not a random set of projected criteria.

I am sure you will agree that, regardless of which solution you implement, there are real savings to be realized. It also meets our goal by:

- Saving operational costs with reduced energy consumption. (Also, potentially reduces maintenance costs as the "run times" may be reduced.)
- Increases efficiency by allowing these systems to set comfort levels without a staff person having to dart from thermostat to thermostat setting and resetting temperatures.
- We are GREAT corporate citizens by reducing energy consumption.
- Operational efficiency soars. We have clients that have implemented one of the above strategies and have seen not only an energy efficiency reduction but an increase in operational efficiency of 20-30%. When you can automate tasks that are currently consuming your staff's time (i.e., turning the temperature up and down in your facility for every event), their efficiency will increase by allowing them to focus on the critical matters of stewarding and caring for the facility.

WIN – WIN – WIN - WIN

Tip #2: Reduce Your Electrical Power Consumption through Lighting

After the cost associated with HVAC, your lighting will likely be the next largest consumer of electricity. If I were a "green radical", I would give you all the facts of how wind-powered energy or solar energy can help you save significant money. And while that is very true, I am not sure it is practical for most churches. In the "for-profit" sectors, there is a significant case to be made for making the switch to alternative energy due in part to the tax credits, tax incentives, and other similar programs that will not benefit a non-profit entity. Given that, allow me to focus on the more practical elements.

Replace inefficient light bulbs. There are so many great options available to us today. I am amazed at what the energy savings can be by simply changing out light bulbs. Several years ago, the rave was to move from incandescent bulbs to Compact Fluorescent (CFL). These CFL bulbs used less energy than their counterpart and lasted longer. At that time, the LED bulb was in its infancy and was very costly. Not any more! Today, if you are not moving to LED's for all your lighting needs, you are just throwing money away. Here are just some of the considerations:

- To obtain the same lumens (brightness) of an incandescent bulb, you need an LED that consumes about 85% less energy;
- An LED bulb can last up to 21 times longer than an incandescent, meaning less operational money both in replacement bulbs and time to replace them; and,
- Many local utility providers are offering significant rebates and incentives for converting your lighting to LED. This can save you a great deal in the initial cost of changing over.

Tip #3: Incorporate Occupancy Sensors

The old term was "motion detectors" as the original technology was designed to detect motion, primarily for security systems. Over the past decade, this technology has become mainstream and is used in a whole host of applications.

Occupancy sensors are ideally suited for applications that require a higher granularity of control than can be economically achieved using scheduling (e.g., a floor of an education or office building with perimeter offices that must be controlled individually). Sensors are most suitable when space is intermittently occupied, meaning it is unoccupied for two or more hours per day, and where the lights are left on when the space is unoccupied. Appropriate applications include offices, classrooms, copy rooms, restrooms, storage areas, conference rooms, break rooms, corridors, filing areas, and other similar spaces. As part of an EPA study, entitled "Demand Reduction and Energy Savings Using Occupancy Sensors," researchers monitored 158 rooms at 60 buildings for occupancy and lighting status over 14 days. They found that occupancy sensors could cut energy waste by up to 68% and increase energy savings by about 60%.[3]

These devices are relatively easy to install, as well as cost-effective. I strongly recommend you use them in any occupy-able space that does not have a window. If you are driving by the facility in the evening and see lights on, you can stop and turn them off. But in internal spaces and areas such as restrooms that do not have windows, these fixtures could stay on all night – what a waste.

Tip #4: Switch from Night to Day Cleaning

This is going to sound very radical, but this is the current trend in office, healthcare, and many other secular settings. Think about it; if you do night cleaning, you are burning lights and keeping the space at a reasonable temperature to clean the facility. With the advanced technology of quiet HEPA vacuums (more on this later) and non-toxic/semi-odorless cleaning products, would it not make sense to make some adjustments to your cleaning patterns? Even if you cannot move all of it to the daytime, what if you incorporated early morning cleaning at a time when there is natural light, and the HVAC systems are already starting to energize for the day? Or even as close to the close of business as possible.

I researched a facility that used ProTeam Quiet Pro Vacuums (http://www.pro-team.com/vacuums/default.aspx). In this case, custodians had been cleaning the building from 6:00 p.m. to 12:00 a.m. The new schedule was adjusted to 7:00 a.m. to 7:00 p.m. with staggered crews. Again, significant savings.

This will require a paradigm shift and will work best if the senior level staff supports it. We can no longer repeat the seven words of a dying church: *We have always done it that way.*

As you can see, you have several options available to reduce your church's utility bills. Even if you're only able to implement one of these tips within the next twelve months, you'll still see a gradual decrease in the monthly utility bill. It's worth the effort to steward the facilities and finances God entrusted to you.

CHAPTER 9

CUSTODIAL: CLEANLINESS IS NEXT TO GODLINESS

One of the least glamorous and often overlooked aspects of ministry is keeping church facilities clean. Seemingly, little things like washing windows (particularly at the entrance), keeping bathrooms well-stocked, and getting scuff marks off the walls can make a great first impression.

Despite the importance of this function, this is an area of Facilities Stewardship where I see the greatest fluctuation and the most turnover in staff/vendors. So, how clean is clean enough? There are so many personal preferences with cleaning and janitorial services that it may be hard to give a real definitive recommendation, but I will try.

In our 2019 Church Facility Operations Benchmarking Assessment, respondents spent roughly $1.11 per square foot on custodial staffing costs. Additionally, we found that churches spend $0.23 per square foot on custodial supplies. You also need to account for paper products, seasonal cleaning, carpet extraction, cleaning equipment purchases/leases, etc. When we add all of these together, the most effective and efficient church facilities are budgeting $1.75 - $2.50 per square foot annually.

If your costs are significantly higher than these averages, it might be time to evaluate how you handle janitorial tasks. I recommend going green. An area often overlooked by church facility operators is the savings related to green cleaning systems, processes, and methodologies. Here are a few tips to consider:

Tip #1: You can't smell clean

You may have heard it said like this, but think about it. Can you smell clean, or are you just smelling the chemicals used to attempt to clean? For most consumers, we have grown accustomed to particular smells that give us comfort that something has been cleaned. Pine-Sol® has promoted this in their ad campaigns for years, but are you really smelling clean? What is "clean" supposed to smell like? This leads me to the second topic…

Tip #2: All cleaning solutions aren't created equal

While it's tempting to purchase the least expensive or the latest trend in cleaning solutions, neither of those methods will get the best results. Instead, you'll need to research what types of cleaning solutions will work well for the different types of surfaces and various conditions that exist within your facilities.

Tip #3: Start backpacking

I am not suggesting a camping trip but rather making the change to backpack vacuums. Backpack vacuum cleaners are lightweight and allow for increased mobility. They can fit in areas where other vacuums do not. They maximize productivity and double the speed of cleaning versus standard upright vacuums.

When you first start researching the possibilities in backpack vacuums, you will encounter a bewildering array of choices, and it seems like the specifications for each don't even relate to one another.

Here's what you should consider when choosing a backpack vacuum solution:

1. Fit – Probably the most important consideration is whether the vacuum fits your body correctly. You need to put it on and have someone help you adjust the straps until it is sitting comfortably. Now, try to bend

over. Does it hit your waist in such a way that it prevents you from bending easily?

2.   Suction – Without a doubt, this is the most difficult thing to evaluate when choosing a vacuum, and unfortunately, there is no standard definition of suction or airflow that all manufacturers use to rate their machines – that would be too easy! The main terms you'll see, and the formulas associated, are:

- Watts
- Peak HorsePower
- Air Flow
- Water Lift
- Air Watts

3.   Filtration – Most backpack vacuums have excellent filtration and are sealed well to keep you from breathing dirty exhaust air close to your nose. With that in mind, you only need to check whether it has three or four-level filtration and if HEPA filters are available. The term HEPA stands for High-Efficiency Particulate Air, and for a filter to be rated as HEPA it must retain all particles .3 microns in size or larger at an efficiency level of 99.97%.

4.   Weight – Most backpack vacuums come in under ten pounds. The weight and size of the dirt canister are going to be a bit of a trade-off.

5.   Noise – Because this type of vacuum is so much closer to your head than a regular vacuum, they are usually not too noisy. The noise rating is generally given in decibels and should be under 70db. The lower the number, the better.

Tip #4: To Mat or Not To Mat

An entrance mat is the first line of defense against contaminants and particles entering the building. As such, an entrance mat should:

- Stop soil and water. 85% of all soil enters a building on the feet of its occupants.[1]

- Store soil and water for removal at a convenient time. "Storing" means that a high-performance mat contains soil in a place where it can be removed effectively and safely with minimum impact on the building. A building with minimized contaminants reduces the number of cleaning chemicals required. This reduces airborne contaminants and volatile organic contaminants (VOCs) from cleaning chemicals, thereby improving a building's Indoor Air Quality (IAQ).

- Minimize the tracking of stored soil and water into the building. A mat with upper and lower surfaces will store soil and water below shoe level to prevent it from being transferred into the building. This is perhaps the most important thing an entrance mat should do. Mats with a non-re-enforced surface will crush flat, and once the soil is deposited on these mats, it can reattach to the shoe of another person and be tracked further into the building.

- Provide a safe surface for traffic. Entrance mats should retain contaminants within the structure of the mat and not allow them to seep onto the floor, causing a potential slip/fall accident. Mats without a rubber reinforced permanent bi-level construction become saturated with water that can cause a loss of traction on the mat or adjacent floor.

The ISSA (International Sanitary Supply Association) estimates that up to 24 pounds of dirt can be tracked into a facility that is visited by 1,000 people over 20 days.[2] As much as 70-80% of dirt is tracked from the outside. During the winter this percentage is much higher. ISSA estimates that it can cost approximately $600 to remove one pound of dirt[2], so the best way to save money in this area is to keep the dirt from entering the building. To be effective, you need to install matting at each entrance, and it needs to be long enough for the average person to step several times.

Tip #5: Choose Green-Certified Cleaning Chemicals

Typically speaking, we spend more hours indoors than outdoors. For this reason, it is important to use cleaning practices that promote good indoor air quality. Green-certified cleaning chemicals should give you the cleaning performance you require while protecting the health of users and building occupants. Your cleaning policy should outline the use of green-certified chemicals whenever possible.

Remember that your choice of cleaning chemicals needs to answer the three basic requirements for an effective green cleaning program:

- The cleaning product must meet your cleaning requirements; you still need to provide a clean facility.
- It must protect the health of the workers and the building occupants.
- It must have a reduced impact on the environment when compared to traditional cleaning chemicals.

How do you know what products are reliable? How do you know these products have been tested and certified by a reputable organization and not just someone claiming to be "green"? Thankfully, you can find several expert organizations that have proven to provide consumers with just this kind of information. This leads me to the next topic…

Tip #6: How to determine what is "green" and what isn't

Several third-party organizations define environmentally preferable ingredients, characteristics, and performance standards on products we use to clean, as well as the buildings we are cleaning. Some of the most prominent and widely accepted guidelines come from these organizations:

- USGBC and LEED® (www.usgbc.org)
- The United States Environmental Protection Agency (EPA.gov)
- EPA Design for the Environment (DfE) (www.epa.gov/saferchoice)
- Green Seal (www.greenseal.org)
- Carpet and Rug Institute Green Label Certification (www.carpet-rug.org)

Tip #7: Use Microfiber Cloths

The Best Thing Since Soap and Water - Yes, it's true! Microfiber cloths are the best thing to happen in the cleaning industry since the most basic of cleaning ingredients came about. Microfiber towels are hands-down the best cleaning product on the market. Better than any spray, wipe, or liquid you can buy. They will not only make your cleaning easier and faster, but you will clean better. This is because microfiber towels clean in ways ordinary products can't.

Here's the rundown. Microfiber towels will make your cleaning easier because they...

- Have electrostatic cleaning. This means that, due to an electrostatic charge, the dust won't just fly away and then redeposit on the screen or desk when you dust your computer screens. The dust is picked up and attracted to the cloth.
- Offer a better cleaning surface than cotton. Microfiber cloths have a waffle-type texture that traps dirt and dust, actually gripping the dirt. This allows you to clean your glass, chrome, or shiny metal surfaces to a bright, shiny gleam without using harsh chemicals. All it requires is a lightly dampened cloth, and you have as much shining and cleaning power as a bucket of ammonia.
- You can wash and reuse it several times. Unlike sponges that you can't wash, or paper towels that you throw away, you can use

microfiber towels repeatedly. Just throw them in the wash with a little detergent, and you have a fresh new cloth. You can reuse most microfiber cloths up to 500 times. Just think about how much you can save in paper towels and other products! The average microfiber cleaning cloth is about three dollars, at 500 uses, that is less than .01 cent per use.

Initially used for car detailing, microfiber towels are finally making their way into facility cleaning closets. There's even a microfiber mop that you can use to make your floors glow. Just give it a mist with some water and then go to town. Since you won't use a lot of water, like damp mopping, you won't damage your floors. Plus, the fine quality of the weave means the mop won't leave behind any smudges or streaks.

I realize this is a ton of data (probably more than you can absorb all at once or maybe more than you ever wanted to know), but the fact remains that we have been entrusted to steward the things God has given to us.

Training

Now, these tips aren't useful unless you put them into practice and that involves your custodial team. Too often, we assume our team knows how to clean. We think that if we provide the right tools, the rest will take care of itself. Nothing could be further from the truth.

Training provides the foundation for the results of what we do. If you are getting less than stellar results, it is because your training is lacking. I find that there is a great deal of truth in a quote attributed to the Greek soldier Archilochus, circa 650 B.C:

"We don't rise to the level of our expectations; we fall to the level of our training."[3]

Here are a few key terms related to proper training:

Term #1: Process

As the word implies, it is a method that has a definable and observable beginning, middle, and end. We do not hand the keys to our 16-year-old and say, "Be careful, don't wreck," and expect that they will be competent drivers. Some people may have (looking at you Dallas), but if we want our teens to be safe drivers, we follow the process of drivers education. It has a beginning (written materials), a middle (practice driving with those that are trained), and an end (final testing at the DMV). At any time in the process, you may have to camp out a bit longer or review.

Term #2: Agreed Standard

This one is big. We can disagree on what color something is, even when we read the description, so how easy is it to have different views on what a "standard" is? This is when reading becomes part of training…write down what the successful completion of a task looks like. Show it to your team and let them refer to it when they want to know if they have done it correctly. If you are leading a team, there is no excuse for you not to put in the extra effort to define your standards.

Term #3: Practice and Instruction

Now you need to teach and observe. Teach team members what you want them to do, watch the progress, correct, and re-train as necessary. This is an ongoing process…but not a process without end. If you have someone that simply cannot achieve the agreed standard, you then have a choice. You can change (lower) the standard to that person's level of capability, or you can change the team member. Sometimes the most gracious act we can do is let underperforming team members go sooner rather than later. It is not easy, but as leaders, it is part of what we are expected to do.

Invest the time now to document proper cleaning procedures, review the documentation with your team, and offer regular training and feedback. This will help your team succeed and will ensure you're excellent stewards of the facilities entrusted to you.

CHAPTER 10
SAFETY ISN'T OVERRATED

In addition to performing preventative maintenance, monitoring utility usage, and keeping church facilities clean, there's another key aspect to stewarding the resources entrusted to you...maintaining a safe environment.

While you can't guarantee everyone's safety 100% of the time, there are practical actions you can take to reduce the likelihood of an accident or injury. In this chapter, we'll address several areas you should regularly monitor to establish and maintain a safe environment for your congregation and community.

The Legal Aspect of Safety

While I'm not an advocate of foul language, there is a four-letter word many consider "bad"...OSHA. At the forefront of improving workplace safety, OSHA came from a desire to see fewer people killed or horrifically injured on the job. Sounds great, right? I, for one, am thankful for New Jersey Senator Harrison A. Williams, Jr. And Representative William A. Steiger, the drivers behind The Occupational Safety and Health Act of 1970, also known as the Williams-Steiger Act. Like any piece of legislation[1], it has morphed over the years in some unfortunate ways. However, the fact remains that keeping people safe at work is a good thing.

So, does OSHA apply to a house of worship? - Yes.

Here are the sections that apply to churches and houses of worship:

- OSHA 1975.4(c) Coverage of churches and special policy as to certain church activities

- 1975.4(c)(1) Churches. Churches or religious organizations, like charitable and non-profit organizations, are considered employers under the Act where they employ one or more persons in secular activities.
- 1975.4(c)(2) Examples. Some examples of coverage of religious organizations as employers would be: A private hospital-owned or operated by a religious organization; a private school or orphanage owned or operated by a religious organization; commercial establishments of religious organizations engaged in producing or selling products such as alcoholic beverages, bakery goods, religious goods, etc.; and administrative, executive, and other office personnel employed by religious organizations.

What does that mean for you?

Primarily, it means there are some particular OSHA regulations you should address. On a deeper level, it means you need to ask yourself how much you value your safety and the safe work environments of those around you. The level at which you value these things is the level at which you will develop, grow, and encourage a culture of safety in your building. Honestly, it is not that hard, but it must be *intentional*. This is a word you will see used a great deal at Smart Church Solutions; what we do is done on purpose and deliberate. Safety is no accident. When my children went to get their driver's licenses, they didn't get to walk into the DMV and say, "Hey guys, I want to drive, how about a license?" They went through months of the classwork and practical driving experience with us. We were intentional about going over the why and the how. They accepted the fact that if they were going to earn a license, safely operating a vehicle was required. It is part of the driving culture we created.

The methodology used to create a culture of safe drivers is similar to the one needed to create a safe culture in your church. While you must stay focused on your mission, it's critical to recognize the role you play in maintaining the safety of those involved in the mission.

The funny thing about safety is that you really cannot force it upon individuals. If establishing rules was all it took to make people responsible, we would have fewer lawyers and insurance agents. Show your team how integral they are to your mission and, in turn, you will have a team that sees the value in safely executing their role.

The Only Fire We Want Involves the Holy Spirit

Fire can cause devastating damage and threaten lives should it sweep through your church facility. Thankfully, there are practical steps you can take to reduce the likelihood of a fire, and the impact should one occur. Let's explore some common causes of church fires, but keep in mind that it is crucial to consider the type of structure to which we are referring. Most church facilities are considered, and should be managed as, commercial buildings.

Common Causes of Structural Fires:

#1: Arson

You might already know that one of the leading causes of commercial fires is arson. Since arson is a deliberate act, it is challenging to create a system that would protect you entirely from someone intent on burning your facility. What we must ensure is that the notification and alerting systems we can have are indeed in place and functioning correctly. If you do not have a sprinkler system, it could be a system worth exploring. There are alternatives to iron pipe for retro-fitting a structure with a sprinkler system. Keep in mind, though, that it could still be costly, and it is only one component of a total system. Check with your local code official, known as the Authority Hiring Jurisdiction (AHJ), to see if some of the non-metallic options are right for you.

#2: Human Error

One of the next prevalent causes of fires in commercial structures is human error. Not surprisingly, we humans do some questionable things. One source of fire that we see a great deal of is those little room freshener candles. Leaving a flame unattended is not the best of ideas, but even the most attentive individual might get up to take care of something and end up away for hours. The light bulb heated scent holders aren't exactly safe either as the surface on these becomes quite hot. Leaving any heat source unattended is not a good idea.

#3: Candles

We could include this one under Human Error, but it bears having its own section. Many denominations utilize candles as part of their worship experience regularly. Generally, those churches will have some basic safety protocols in place. However, others may only use candles occasionally, such as during a Christmas Eve candlelight service.

Infrequent candle use can increase the likelihood of accidents in your facility. Two types of events seem to feature the sudden use of lit candles: weddings and Christmas services.

Many times, in addition to a unity candle or the like, couples will have tea candles or votives throughout the worship center. It makes a pretty backdrop for pictures and the ceremony but makes facility managers nervous. Christmas will bring forth the ever-popular candlelight service, or as I fondly refer to it, the "I hope when everyone blows out their candle, it does not set off the fire alarm" service. With these specific events, or any intermittent use of candles in your facility, there are some simple steps you can take to be safe.

First of all, keep in mind that quality matters. When choosing your candle, you should look for the best quality available. The better the candle, the slower and more controlled the burn rate. Faster-burning candles will create more wax quickly and potentially generate higher flames. Those things combined can make a candle for the candlelight service more fitting for storming a castle than for worship. Also, make sure that hand-held candles have a fully enclosed wax catcher on the candle, not just the little paper slide shields. We know we are going to have to clean wax off the seating, but at least we can try and minimize it. It also helps keep sudden contact with hot wax a less than likely occurrence.

Someone should give instruction on the appropriate use of hand-held candles. Take the time to remind folks that the lit candles should always remain upright, tip the unlit candles into the flame of the lit candle. Remind parents to monitor their children closely. And while the hairstyles of the '80s and '90s were a bit scarier, it is good to remind folks that hair is particularly flammable.

Also, consider the placing of stationary candles. Try to avoid areas that have a frequent influx of air (around doorways and HVAC supplies) as well as areas near main routes of travel. Ensure that there is an adequate amount of space from the candle to all surrounding flammable areas (to the bottom of the candle holder as well). Try only to use purpose-made candle holders for all your candle placements.

Check to make sure that you have enough fire extinguishers available in the area where you are utilizing candles. If you do not typically use candles in the area, it may be a good idea to bring in a couple of extra extinguishers. In addition to having them available, consider training and placing some individuals near them to be ready to use them if the need arises.

In addition to extinguishers, a fire blanket could be useful in the event an individual is in danger. Smothering the flames may be more effective than trying to get them with an extinguisher. Again, taking the time to have someone ready, trained, and willing to perform the task if needed, is important here.

While these measures may sound like overkill, as stewards of our church facilities and the people within them, we are called to anticipate the unusual and have a plan to mitigate it.

#4: Cooking

The next (preventable) cause is cooking fires. Having food in our facility is a common occurrence. Many churches have large commercial grade equipment in their kitchen areas. The danger is that commercial equipment is not generally the same as residential. There can be a learning curve when using a commercial-grade range for the first time. For example, if you have a range that requires a vent-hood, it's important to make sure that everyone who uses the kitchen knows: 1) that they must turn it on and 2) how to turn it on. It is not as intuitive as you might think. Safety devices are only effective if they are used and used correctly.

#5: Heating

Winter involves the reason for the next cause, heating. We hope that everyone is doing proper preventative maintenance of all their HVAC equipment. Unfortunately, many facility managers only check the heating when they turn it on for the first time. This can lead to unsafe conditions and even fires. During the cooling season, we may block venting or allow flammable items to be stored too close to the burner. It is not unusual to have a "burning" smell the first time you fire up a gas heater as it is burning off the dust that has settled. It is a good idea to check them and make sure it is just dust. The heating season also means the use of personal heaters. While some are safe, many times they can have exposed heating elements that can cause burns, ignite flammable material, or overload circuits.

#6: Electrical

Overloaded circuits and improperly rated extension cords are the culprits here. A lack of available outlets is a common occurrence in facilities. Unfortunately, we tend to add power strips and extension cords without carefully considering the potential ramifications. Extension cords should only be as long as needed since curled up cords can lead to overheating. Power-strips should only have the number of devices plugged into them that do not exceed the maximum amperage of the circuit and should have the ability to cut themselves off if they become overloaded or experience a surge.

Short of arson, we can reduce other common causes of commercial structural through positive engagement by your people in the building. Take the time to walk through your facility and look for areas that are at risk. Then take the steps to mitigate that risk.

Are You Sure that Fire Extinguisher Will Work in an Emergency?

We see them all the time. In entertainment (television and movies), the hero tends to use them as a means of defense. Most of us will never need to utilize one in our lifetime. I am, of course, referring to a portable fire extinguisher.

When we talk about portable fire extinguishers, OSHA and the National Fire Protection Association (NFPA) are your best friends. Both organizations offer significant resources for you and your facility. Remember, if you have them, then the expectation is that you intend for staff to use them. If you intend for staff to use them, then you need to train them.

Here are a few key points you need to know about fire extinguishers:

#1 - What fires can it put out?

First, when looking at an extinguisher, it is important to know what class of fire it is capable of fighting along with your current need.

Different classes are as follows:

- A (ordinary combustibles like wood, paper, trash, and plastic)
- B (flammable liquid or gas as the fuel base)
- C (electrical equipment/energized source as the fuel source)

- D (combustible metals)
- K (fires that have cooking oils as their fuel source).

Knowing the class of fire you may experience allows you the opportunity to make sure you have the right extinguisher.

#2 - What size is it?

Size is vital in extinguishers. The number you see before the letter A equates to the water equivalency, which is the number multiplied by 1.25. The number before the letter B indicates the square footage of coverage. A portable fire extinguisher rated at 10B would cover 10 square feet of a class B fire if used properly. There is not a number associated with C or D class extinguishers. An extinguisher rated for C should be able to handle the A or B component of the fire, and a class D extinguisher will be rated based on the type of metal it is recommended for.

#3 - Where are they?

Location, location, location. There are many different measurements and distances you can find for how often you should see a fire extinguisher. On average, you are looking at a travel distance somewhere between 50 to 100 feet. That means someone would not need to travel farther than that distance to access the extinguisher. The class of fire will determine how close an extinguisher should be. Type K extinguishers are a bit unique, as they must be located directly next to, or within six feet, of the potential fire source. In a commercial kitchen, the vent hood will most likely have a type K agent able to be released directly on the cooking equipment with a secondary type K extinguisher mounted on another wall in the kitchen.

Other considerations with location are mounting height, visibility, and accessibility. Extinguishers should be mounted so the top is between three and a half to five feet off the floor (depending on weight). They should be easily accessible on the main (or primary) routes of travel in your facility. The only extinguishers that should be on the floor are the ones that have permanently affixed wheels. You may also need to provide a secondary sign above the extinguisher alerting folks to its presence, such as a red and white sticker that has an arrow with a "fire extinguisher" label.

#4 - Who knows how to use it?

Another aspect of an intentional portable fire extinguisher program is training. If you expect or intend your staff to utilize a fire extinguisher, when appropriate, you are required to train them. A typical training program will go over the things necessary for a fire to occur, explain the different classes of extinguishers and what types of fires they are for, the proper way to engage a fire with a portable fire extinguisher, and how to inspect the extinguishers. This training should be done upon initial hiring and annually after that.

#5 - How do you know it will work?

Portable fire extinguishers need to be certified annually by a licensed company. They will also be able to perform the required hydrostatic and other specialized testing/certifications when they are due. In addition to the annual inspections, you should perform monthly checks.

If you don't already have a policy and plan established to ensure proper maintenance and usage of fire extinguishers, today is a great day to get started. While I hope you never need to use one, if you find yourself in an emergency situation, you'll be grateful you invested the time to ensure they're working correctly, they're easy to reach, and people know how to use them.

As you develop or review your fire extinguisher operations, go to http://www.smartchurchsolutions.com/entrustedresources and download the Fire Extinguisher Plan for a template to start with or compare against.

Handling Chemicals Safely

SDS, which stands for Safety Data Sheet, is the name of the document that replaced MSDS (Material Safety Data Sheets). The change happened in 2012, with an implementation date of all the new requirements by June of 2016. Safety Data Sheets are a component of a proper Hazardous Communication Program (hereafter referred to as HazCom) that every facility should have in place. Unfortunately, the second most cited standard by OSHA in fiscal year 2018 was for failures in HazCom.[2] The overall purpose of HazCom is not to be a formidable addition to your facility world. The intent is to help make sure all occupants in your facility are well protected when it comes to the chemicals in use at your facility.

When it comes to a proper HazCom program, there are five essential parts.

1. Written program

2. Proper labels

3. Correct SDS's

4. Provide training

5. Maintain an accurate inventory

Several of these parts take time to do correctly, but there is not a massive training component to become proficient in them. Creating a chemical inventory is as simple as going through every part of your facility (cabinets, cubbies, storerooms, etc.) and recording the name and manufacturer of every chemical you find. These are not just cleaning chemicals. Hand sanitizer, fragrance sprays, glue, air freshener plug-ins…these are all chemicals. Once you have done that (I guarantee there are more chemicals in your facility than you realize), put the information in a spreadsheet and sort it alphabetically by product name. This will help you with the SDS part of HazCom. At that point, you will know all the SDS that you need to procure and have on hand. These can be stored electronically or in hard copy; the main thing is that they must be easily and readily accessible. Put them in a binder in alphabetical order, using your chemical inventory sheet as the table of contents.

The preceding takes care of two of the five components of a HazCom program. Getting the proper labels for the chemicals is also very straight forward, assuming you are willing to require it. If you are using a dilution control system (and you probably should be), the chemical supplier will and should be able to provide for you the appropriate labels to put on the secondary chemical containers. You can make your own or even write them on the container, but factory-produced is much better. If you are buying chemicals at the big box stores, only use them in their original packaging; do not put chemicals in unlabeled containers.

Pretty simple...three out of the five requirements knocked out. Unfortunately, many organizations stop at that point and venture no further. Your HazCom program is inadequate without the documentation or the training component. Those two parts are necessary if you want your people to be safe.

The written program does not have to be crazy; it needs a list of chemicals present/in use, information on where the SDS are located, labeling standards, and what training you offer. Training is simple as well. A proper training program occurs before folks work with chemicals, when new chemicals are introduced, or when new routines are introduced. Training should include how to safely work with chemicals (think safe handling, Personal Protective Equipment, spill control), and where to find and how to understand SDS.

As you can see, a proper HazCom program is not as difficult as you think yet can help keep your people and facilities safe.

The Sermon Begins in the Parking Lot

That's a quote by Andy Stanley,[3] and it makes a lot of sense. Guests will start to develop their first impression of your church based on what they see and experience in the parking lot. If the lot is full of potholes, if the lines are difficult to see, and if you have weeds growing through cracks all over the lot, that will leave a poor first impression.

Assuming your church has a parking lot around the facility, most will be asphalt parking lots. Without proper maintenance, asphalt lots will deteriorate, be very unsightly, and dangerous. So how do we keep that from happening?

A typical asphalt parking lot should have the following components: a subgrade (existing soil/material), an aggregate (drainage) layer, a base layer, and a final surface layer. Thicknesses will depend on expected traffic patterns and location. The preceding was the professional ideal; what I have seen in many churches is a layer of compacted fill followed by a 1-2-inch layer of asphalt.

This may explain why many of us have experienced issues with our parking lots, especially if our activity level has increased. So, let's go through some common issues and how you can repair them. (You can do much of this in-house.)

Issue #1: Small cracking

This is the first sign of wear and tear. Repairing these immediately is crucial because left unchecked they will lead to larger issues. Fortunately, it is cheap, quick, and easy to fix them at this stage. To repair a crack, all you need is something to blow out the crack, a squeegee, and a commercial-grade liquid crack filler. Clean the crack out (sweep then blow it out), apply enough liquid crack filler directly in the crack that it comes to the top, and squeegee the crack when it is full to level out the extra. You may notice that the next day the filler has sunk in a bit, if so, add a bit more filler.

Issue #2: Alligatoring

These are the cracks that did not get filled when they were tiny and have spread and broadened to resemble alligator skin. You will need tools to clean/blow off the surface, a trowel, a squeegee, and a commercial alligator patch (pourable patch repair). Clean and prep the surface, then apply the patch material according to the manufacturer's instructions. Alligator patch will have a mix of binding agents and small aggregate to fill in and bridge the damaged areas. Some products even come with fine black sand to help you blend the patch in.

Issue #3: Potholes

These are a bit more involved to do, but you can still do it if they are small. Tools needed can include a saw with a diamond or asphalt blade, safety gear, hand compactor, liquid sealer, and cold-patch asphalt patch. Cold patch, like the name implies, does not need to be heated up. I like to cut lines around the area I am patching as a straight vertical line when filling a hole creates a better surface to build to. Once you've removed the old material, spend some time re-compacting the base. Once it is compacted, patch with the cold patch. Some manufacturers recommend putting down a thin layer of sealer after application to help keep water out. This works for areas that are between 1-2 inches deep.

Larger issues than those, you probably need to consider working with a contractor. Ponding and rutting are more advanced repair processes. Re-striping or refreshing your parking lot lines can be done with a variety of tools.

The Deadly Weapon We Use Daily

What is this weapon? It's your vehicle. Driving to work or school isn't a significantly dangerous endeavor. Unfortunately, between distracted and impatient drivers, serious injuries or fatalities are possible. That's just with your personal vehicle. What about the larger vans often used for transporting to and from church activities? During the summer months, the demand on church-owned vehicles increases. Unfortunately, many churches just fuel vehicles when needed, get them registered and inspected each year, and hope it's an easy fix when they break.

Instead of that approach, we're going to think a little deeper on this topic and mention the Federal Motor Carrier Safety Administration. If you have a vehicle designed to carry 16 or more people, including the driver, there are some requirements that you may not be aware of. Vehicles that size are generally going to be procured from a bus manufacturer and will require a Commercial Driver's License (CDL) to operate. There are also requirements from the Federal Motor Carrier Safety Administration (FMCSA) that you should be know about. Assuming you are not charging folks to use the vehicles and making a profit, you are going to be classified as a Private Motor Carrier of Passenger, Non-Business. This is important, because it exempts you from many, though not all, of commercial motor vehicle requirements. You may need a Department of Transportation (DOT) number if you cross state lines, or even if you never leave the state depending on your state's rules. You will also have some record-keeping requirements, including a drug and alcohol testing program.

Churches can operate vehicles for many years without realizing they need to comply, and, sadly, they won't know it until they are given fines by the (FMCSA) after an accident. If you operate a vehicle that falls under the jurisdiction of the FMCSA, and it is involved in an accident that they investigate (an accident involving death, serious injury, or destruction of any vehicle involved, or some other criteria) then you could face additional fines. Ignorance of the need provides no absolution.

Hopefully, you already knew this, or you do not operate vehicles that fall under the FMCSA jurisdiction. For the smaller vehicles, there still are "best practices" that you need to consider. Preventative maintenance must be a priority. Part of preventative maintenance needs to include driving that vehicle regularly - just to get it out on the road. Of course, this would be without passengers as it is a vehicle operational check. Preventative maintenance of vehicles also includes annual inspections, regular oil changes, tire rotation, washing the exterior, and cleaning the interior. Driving the vehicle and cleaning it regularly allows you to find operational conditions that are occurring before using the vehicle on a trip.

Unless you are an organization that can afford to have a paid staff member do all the driving, many times you utilize volunteers to drive your vehicles on trips. We must remember that we are putting a driver into the worst conditions on these trips. We're asking them to drive a vehicle they are not used to driving all the time, with a load of passengers that may be loud and distracting. Participating in ministry trips includes a common theme, which is how tired and drained we get. The emotional highs and lows are intense. Fatigued, distracted driving in an unfamiliar vehicle, on routes not commonly driven, can be as dangerous as being on the road with an impaired driver. Considering how incredibly precious our cargo is, these situations require that we take the time to make sure our vehicles, and our drivers, are in the best shape possible.

If you don't have these established already, make sure you develop the following as soon as possible:

- A policy regarding who is authorized to drive church vehicles and the criteria people must obtain before applying to operate a church vehicle (clear background and driving records, proof of current driver's license, etc.).
- A policy regarding who may transport individuals for church activities in a personal vehicle.
- Maintenance schedule for all church-owned vehicles with proof of completed maintenance.
- Record of insurance for all church-owned vehicles.

- Record of liability insurance related to the usage of church-owned vehicles or usage of personal vehicles for church-related purposes.

The goal here isn't to add paperwork or to keep people from participating in church activities. However, it is your responsibility to ensure that the individuals entrusted to operate a vehicle have a track record of doing so safely. Use these policies and practices to reduce the likelihood of an accident as well as liability exposure for the church.

Facility Equipment that Can Save Lives

An Automated External Defibrillator or AED is a vital tool to have available for cases of sudden cardiac arrest (SCA). Why is an AED important? In circumstances that warrant defibrillation, for every minute a heartbeat is not restored, the chance of survival can decrease by seven to ten percent. To be clear, these are instances that a shock will help. How do you know if that is the case? Modern AED's will analyze the rhythm through the pads and determine it for you. If the device does not recommend a shock, that is when performing compression-only CPR is warranted.

When you consider and add in an AED, there are some things to consider. One, is it manufactured from a reliable company? Look for recognizable brands or seek out recommendations from your local emergency responders. Take a gander at what the local clinic or hospital may have on their wall for an AED.

Make sure that the "consumables" for your AED are readily available. Consumables for AED's include the batteries, the adult pads, and the pediatric pads. These items will require replacement at some time, either due to use or expiration dates.

There are other items you should consider having with your AED. A well-marked storage cabinet is great, along with proper and visible signage. Gloves, scissors, a safety razor, and a mask are all good items to have available as well. To place the pads, you may need to cut away a shirt. Gloves and a mask help protect you from fluids, and a razor could be necessary if you have to apply pads to someone with body hair as that can interfere with the operation of pads.

There is more we could talk about, but the bottom line is that an AED will allow non-medical personnel, with minimal training, to render aid to someone experiencing SCA. It is a safe medical device to deploy with training available from a variety of resources. Having one just makes sense.

CHAPTER 11

A MEASURED APPROACH TO CHURCH SECURITY

We all want people to feel safe, secure, and "at home" in our church facilities. Unfortunately, real-world events remind us that security isn't guaranteed even in houses of worship. While we can't prevent all security issues, there are practical steps you can take to reduce the likelihood of an incident and reduce the number of lives lost should one occur.

I'm a stickler for definitions, and security is no exception. I define security as this: *Any policy, procedure, action, or physical installation designed to keep occupants free from harm as it pertains to the intentionally harmful actions of others. The key part of the definition is "intentionally harmful actions of others."* Security then is all that we do and use to keep the bad actor from doing bad things.

These three areas make up a proper security plan:

1. Policies and procedures - These provide clear standards and directions to anyone involved in the security plan (including volunteers).

2. Equipment - These are the tools your church leadership may decide to use to secure your facilities.

3. Personnel - You must provide the right people with information and training on the policies and procedures for those to be effective. They'll also need training on the security equipment you choose to deploy.

These areas are listed in this order intentionally. While all three are necessary for a proper plan, each builds upon the foundation of the preceding. Equipment and personnel are not sustainable unless you build them on a solid foundation of policies and procedures.

One important point: Before you start implementing the following tips, consider talking with your church leadership team about your "WHY." What do you mean when you say you want your facility to be "secure"? What steps are you willing to take to achieve that goal? What steps are you NOT willing to take? What security posture would your staff and congregation accept?

Laying a Firm Security Foundation with Policies & Procedures

The first step in developing your church's security plan is to create or evaluate your security policies and procedures. Now, I can hear the collective groan already. Unless you are "that person" you probably don't view policies and procedures positively. Ineffective policies and procedures are burdensome; well thought out and implemented policies and procedures provide a firm foundation for all aspects of an organization.

Policies and procedures that are truly useful contain four components. They are:

1. Understandable

2. Trainable

3. Executable

4. Flexible

Component #1: Understandable

Churches, regardless of size, rely on volunteers for many of the roles needed for events and services. These volunteers want to serve, but you may not have volunteers who are well-trained in security. Even if you did, they might not know how your church leadership team chooses to handle security. As a result, you need to write policies in such a way that everyone can understand, regardless of their background.

Component #2: Trainable

Even after volunteers understand why you have a policy in place, they need training on how to carry out that policy. The question is whether you can easily train them to perform the required response to an incident. Your policies need to have achievable goals for the volunteers to accomplish when confronted with a security-related situation.

Component #3: Executable

This is very similar to trainable. It refers to the complexity of response. The more complicated you make a response to a stressful situation, the more difficult it becomes to execute. If given a choice, we tend to choose the easier path. Unfortunately, if the situation is stressful enough, we may not have a choice.

Performing complex tasks is more difficult under stress. To overcome that challenge, you'll need to train under as close to stressful conditions as feasible.

Component #4: Flexible

Flexible, in relation to security policies, does not mean you have flexibility as to whether you will follow the policy. Flexible means you are serious and intentional about your policies and will review them regularly to make any changes as needed.

A security policy should include a statement of intent and define the roles and responsibilities of responsible parties.

These policies should reflect the complexity of your programs and how you do church. For example, if you have one service a week and meet at no other time, your risk is limited. A program that has a private school, several meetings a week, hundreds of staff members, and multiple campuses has a much larger exposure to risk. Both examples have risks that leadership should address, and the plan should match that level of risk. Over-complicating your policies or adding procedures that do not match your context, or are too hard to understand, will reduce the sustainability of your security plan.

So what are you to do with this information? Here are four practical next steps (assuming you already have your "WHY" identified as recommended at the beginning):

Step #1: Review your current security-related policies and procedures

- Consider whether your current policies and procedures support your "WHY."
- Seek advice and review from legal counsel and your church's insurance provider.
- Consider asking local first responders to review your policies and procedures and offer their expert input.
- Ask staff members or volunteer leaders who are unfamiliar with these documents to read them and provide you with feedback. They may point out sections that are unclear or mention situations you didn't address within the latest draft.
- If you have training materials for those required to carry out these policies and procedures, review these and determine if you need to make any changes.
- Decide when to provide a refresher course and new training for applicable staff and volunteers.

Step #2: Update or add security-related policies and procedures as needed

- Talk with other church leaders or subject matter experts regarding the policies and procedures you already have in place. Ask if they recommend adding any policies or procedures.

- Once you've changed or added to the current set of policies and procedures, have legal experts and other third-parties review them as well.

Step #3: Develop a training program

- Create and update training materials based on the applicable policies and procedures.
- Determine who needs training and what material needs to be covered.
- Develop and implement a training schedule.

Step #4: Revisit security-related policies and procedures annually

- Consider any changes in your facilities (new/remodeled areas), church leadership, and culture. Address those changes in the policy and procedure documents.

Building Upon the Foundation with Proper Equipment

Once you've defined the "WHY" regarding your church's security plans, and you've developed your policies and procedures, it's time to discuss what equipment can complement your plan and help carry out those actions.

Regardless of the size or nature of your church facility, there is a distinct advantage to the well-thought-out planning of the security equipment you'll use. The right equipment allows for an increased security presence without needing additional personnel. Not every church can afford a dedicated security team. However, churches of all sizes can create a more robust security environment with the strategic use of equipment.

Here are several types of equipment you can use to implement your church's security plan:

Equipment Type #1: Locks

You likely have at least one lock on your facility. With some exceptions, the only way to find out who has keys to your building(s) is to change the locks without telling anyone and wait for the angry phone calls.

While that image may have brought a slight smile to your face, the reality is that "key possession" highlights one of the challenges churches face in implementing access control. Many individuals may feel they can be trusted and need a key to take care of something in the facility they are passionate about. Regardless of their noble intentions, reducing the number of keys in circulation is not a trust issue, it's a security issue. Controlling access to keys helps reduce the likelihood of your facility becoming unsecured without your knowledge.

Equipment Type #2: Threat Notification Systems

"Threat notification systems" is a fancy way of saying alarm systems, i.e., burglar and fire alarms. While there are some systems you can purchase and install on your own, this is an area we recommend partnering with a licensed and qualified contractor in your area. These systems tend to be complicated, and many states have specific requirements on life-safety or security systems in a commercial building. That said, you should still make sure you understand every aspect of your system. If a vendor wants to install a system they cannot explain to you, seek another vendor.

While the basic functions of fire and burglar alarms are familiar, there are additional options available that can improve your security plan. For example, panic buttons can be part of many burglar systems.

Equipment Type #3: Cameras

Camera systems are readily available. Pricing for systems ranges from a couple hundred dollars to several thousand. When considering cameras, there are some basic things to keep in mind.

#1: Resolution

Camera options are analog or IP (Internet Protocol). Analog cameras have a limitation to the clarity they can capture while IP cameras are continually improving.

#2: Storage

When considering a camera system, storage is key. Monitoring cameras 24/7 is difficult, and in many instances, the role of camera systems is to determine what happened after an incident. Cameras make great witnesses because they simply show you what they observed. When it comes to storage, more is better.

#3: Network

One advantage of IP cameras is that they can be placed anywhere in your facility where a network connection is available. A potential disadvantage is that it may require a network upgrade to handle the increased streaming load.

#4: Placement

When considering cameras, you need to evaluate what you want the cameras to see and the environment you want to see things in. It is a good practice to consider and confirm environmental conditions (such as the timing of sunlight, etc.) when placing cameras. This means if Sunday morning is your most critical concern, walk around and take notes on the environment and people flow in the areas you want to monitor.

Equipment Type #4: Access Control Systems

Access Control Systems do what the name implies - control an individual's access to an area of the facility. Examples include security badges, key fobs, and access codes. There are a variety of access control systems available, but for any system, you need to consider how they communicate and how they secure. When exploring these systems, consider the type of software they use and fail-safe/secure features.

Equipment Type #5: Communication Devices

In a security situation, you may need to communicate to everyone within the facility, with first responders, and with your security team. Here are a few options:

#1: Cell phones

These are the cornerstone of many emergency communication plans. While they are prevalent, it shouldn't be the only part of your communication plan.

#2: Building intercom systems

This option used to be cost-prohibitive, but as technology improves costs come down. Now, there are many options available from traditional push-to-talk to master stations to VoIP options.

#3: Radios

Radios allow communication to continue in the more extreme scenarios. As long as the radio has power, it will send and receive on the frequency to which it is programmed.

Supported by a Firm Foundation

Personnel is part of a proper security plan. To have a sustainable and effective role for staff, you need to have the appropriate foundation of policies and procedures and equipment. Within the personnel context, it is necessary to understand that there are multiple roles available in a well-executed security plan. In this section, I'll address some standard roles, starting from outside the facility and working our way inside.

Role #1: Parking Lot Monitor

Our first personnel role to consider is the parking lot monitor. This can be as simple as someone willing to sit in your parking lot and keep an eye on things or as involved as a parking lot ministry that assists in directing traffic while providing an initial touch-point for guests. This outer ring can play an essential role in your security plan.

Role #2: Door Greeter

Next, we encourage you to consider the role a door greeter plays. From a welcoming standpoint, we want to make sure people receive a warm smile and have the door opened for them. However, with a proper training program, the initial greeter can provide much more. On the surface, they can provide a welcome service. The reality is they can become a critical security point for your facility.

Role #3: Usher

As you move closer to the main worship area, a familiar role is evident - the usher. We tend to view ushers as handing out bulletins, opening doors, and maybe even passing the plate. Those are all legitimate functions, but just like with door greeters, there is more they can provide.

As you are training personnel, train your ushers on how to deal with disruptive individuals.

Train them on identifying items and individuals that do not pass the "smell test." Train them, train them, train them. One of the best and easiest advantages to having a well-trained usher team is the fact that no one gets super nervous seeing an usher standing up or walking around during service. Use that to your advantage when designing your security plan.

Role #4: Children's Area Helpers

Children's area helpers are great to have any time you are providing care for little ones. These individuals have a dual function--they can help deliver supplies or pass needs of the classrooms to leadership as well as offer mobile security observation. Train your helpers to pay close attention to their territory to increase security.

Role #5: Medical Team

Creating a team of medical personnel is one area church leaders do not always consider. While "Dial 911" is an appropriate response to every emergency, having a dedicated team of volunteers that focus on emergency medical needs is helpful. If you do not have any trained medical personnel in your church, find training programs for those who are willing to learn. Always call 911, but have a planned response until they arrive.

Role #6: Armed Security Personnel

There are many ways to have an armed security presence. Some churches can afford to hire off-duty police officers. Some can afford both uniformed and plainclothes private security. Others rely on members that carry concealed. The most important consideration is to have an honest assessment as to whether you are prepared to have an armed response capability within your facility.

Before we go further, please consider this: When you ask someone to be willing to be armed as part of your security plan, you are asking them to be prepared to potentially kill another individual. This is fundamental and should not be taken lightly. As a company, Smart Church Solutions does not provide consulting in this area. We are not "anti-gun," in fact, most of our team owns guns. However, we have taken the position that we, as a company, are not ready to promote the concept of asking a church volunteer to place themselves in a position to make a life or death decision. There are many excellent organizations that offer training in this area.

I hope you realize this just exposes the very beginning of the process that makes up a security plan. My encouragement to you is to evaluate your current security position and begin improving where you can. Consider the Department of Homeland Security and their national campaign of, "If you see something, say something™"[1]; it is a simple statement that begins the process of engaging communities in taking an active role in their security. Every step you take, regardless of how far it goes, is one step closer to a more secure facility.

SECTION 3: STAFFING - WHO'S GOING TO GET ALL THIS STUFF DONE?

With all that's involved in identifying and coordinating preventative maintenance, keeping facilities clean, handling repairs, implementing safety and security plans, and ensuring everything is ready for events and weekend services, it's easy to see this is a team effort. Regardless of the size of your church facility, this isn't a "one-man show." So, how many people do you need, and in what roles? That's undoubtedly going to vary based on the size and complexity of your facilities. However, there are a few guiding principles I can offer to help you make that determination. Let's dive in.

CHAPTER 12

THE ROLE OF A FACILITY MANAGER

The leader of any church facility management team is the Facility Manager. This individual shouldn't be the one doing all the repair work, maintenance, and cleaning on his/her own. The purpose of this role is to have someone who can keep an eye on the big picture, identify the scope of work, and coordinate the logistics to make it happen.

Before we get into any details on the Facility Manager role, let's address the difference between maintenance and management. Maintenance involves the day-to-day work of fixing toilets, replacing a cracked window, or dealing with an overloaded electrical outlet. The Facility Manager should not perform that work. Instead, someone on his team should handle those issues as assigned. The Facility Manager should be the one monitoring each month's scheduled maintenance and inspecting the work completed. The Facility Manager should talk with the leaders of each ministry area to discuss upcoming events they have planned and ensure facility plans are ready to support each. He should review the preventative maintenance schedule for each asset (HVAC, roof, etc.) and confirm that all preventative maintenance is occurring as needed. Note that these are 30,000-foot view activities and not hands-on task completion activities. The Facility Manager needs the time to keep track of the overall health and upkeep of the church's facilities. It's nearly impossible to do that effectively if he's also responsible for performing all that work as well.

Unfortunately, in most churches, they believe they have a Facility Manager when they actually have a facility maintenance person. This means the business administrator, executive pastor, or a trustee are serving as the Facility Manager with all of their other responsibilities. This also means that this area is not at the front of anyone's mind. Therefore vital tasks may get overlooked or completely ignored.

Unlike some professions, Facility Management encompasses many different roles and skills. Not everyone in the facility or property management profession is responsible for all of these roles. Some are responsible for specific functions as specialists; others are responsible for everything while some oversee all these roles through other specialists. Regardless, it's important to have a working knowledge of each one so you can effectively deal with your colleagues, manage staff, or interface with external resources.

A pie-shaped diagram is the easiest way to represent the broad responsibilities in the Facility Management profession since FM includes so many different skills and duties. This pie graph, which comes directly from the book Managing Facilities & Real Estate, shows the full range of FM responsibilities.

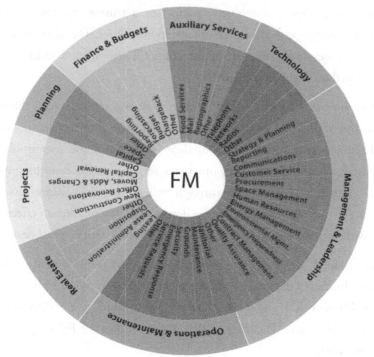

Copyright 2011 Michel Theriault, www.strategicadvisor.ca

"You could categorize them or subdivide them differently, but the fundamental responsibilities are all within this diagram. Depending on your role, you may be responsible for all these elements or just a few. You may also oversee them all, but have other experts on your team who focus on a specific aspect of the role. Some of these specific areas are actually represented by their own professions when performed as a distinct, separate role. For instance, a portion of the chart covers both Commercial Property Management and Project Management. The Facility Management profession actually encompasses both of those functions.

From this, you can see that it is impossible for any given FM to have all the knowledge and skills to perform all the roles that are frequently expected of them. In addition, many of the responsibilities are non-technical, and they are in fact increasingly becoming strategic in nature. That's why a Facility Manager has to rely on other experts, whether on their staff or as contractors and consultants. The profession of Facility Management isn't just about the person with the Facility Manager title – it's also about the large supporting cast of specialists, experts and other professionals.

The Facility Manager's most useful skills are management and leadership related – particularly the ability to develop strategy, communicate, lead a team, and manage resources. The top facility managers in any large company rose to their level because of those skills." - Michel Theriault[1]

The church world, however, doesn't think in these terms (as much as I believe it should). I get the sense that in most churches, the facility manager — or the operations manager — is the lowest position on the organizational chart and the first to get cut if the budget gets too tight. I have visited several church facility managers' offices (if you can really call them that) over the past several years. Some were large, caged spaces — some of them actually "fenced in" with chain link — in boiler rooms. Others were corners of leftover space, with no windows, in basements or storage rooms, and so on. Is this how to treat someone whom you've asked to steward millions of dollars' worth of Kingdom assets? I wouldn't want my office to reside in one of these spaces. Maybe I'm just picky — but perhaps not. Have you spent a day in the facility manager's office at your church? Did your clothes feel dirty when you got out of the chair? Probably. The same chair likely had paint cans stacked on it before you sat down.

Do we think that the facility manager is less critical to the ministry's success than the youth pastor? Is this role less critical than that of the small groups minister? What about the accounting staff? If you said "no" to any of these questions, then why treat the facility manager like a second-class citizen? Facilities represent a large part of any church's assets and expenses; yet, they don't usually receive the same attention as other parts of the organization. While I agree that facilities are only a tool, they're a tool that requires care and stewarding.

Here are several reasons why a church needs a facility management professional:

Reason #1: Facilities are one of your church's largest assets.

They represent a high cost of ongoing operations. A facility management professional has the knowledge to maximize value and minimize costs.

Reason #2: Facilities impact the church environment.

For staff, members, and the congregation-at-large, processes and systems have a massive impact on ministry productivity. A facility management professional understands the church's mission and the interaction with the facility necessary to maximize ministry.

Reason #3: Facility accommodations require strategic planning to minimize costs and maximize value.

Whether the church is in growth mode or not, a facility management professional provides strategic direction and developmental guidance to achieve the results the church needs to fulfill its mission.

Reason #4: Sustainability is critical to the environment, the church, and its members — as well as to community image.

A facility management professional provides the stewardship required to maintain leadership in the environment.

Reason #5: The environmental and legislative complexity of owning or leasing facilities represents a huge risk to the church.

A facility management professional navigates the requirements and mitigates the risk.

Reason #6: Facilities require an entire team of generalists and specialists to provide services.

A facility management professional understands how to make these resources work together to maximize value, reduce risk, and minimize costs.

Reason #7: The facilities that house your ministry can require considerable effort to manage effectively.

A facility management professional takes on this burden and frees up other resources to fully focus on what makes the church successful in delivering its core ministry (Acts 6:1-7).

Reason #8: Managing facilities with an administrative resource or line manager (i.e., maintenance person) means it won't get the attention it deserves — and might put the church at risk.

A facility management professional has training, background, and experience in all areas of the complex issues and services required to provide safe, effective stewardship to the church's facility assets.

Reason #9: A facility management professional has the experience and overall oversight required for facility issues.

This enables them to see patterns, track changes, and identify risks that might have a future negative impact. Their knowledge enables them to take the corrective action necessary to reduce your risk and costs.

Reason #10: Facilities tell a story that the Facility Manager can help craft

Have you ever walked into a restaurant that you read about online or someone recommended…full of anticipation and excitement…only to be turned off by the lack of care of the facility? I have been disappointed more times than I can list when I was in a mid to upper priced establishment, to then visit their restroom and be totally repulsed by the lack of care and cleanliness, or to look up at their ceilings (this is a habit for me, so if you invite me to your facility, know I am looking at your ceilings…you have been warned) to see stained ceiling tiles…or worse…dirty HVAC grills and cobwebs. What does that say about you and your church? What does it say about what you value? Obviously, not the health and well being of your guests and occupants if you are okay allowing dirt and dust to blow down on their heads or have them breathe dirty air.

What story is that telling?

To me, it indicates that either you do not care about your facilities, you are not intentional about their care, or you are in a bad financial condition to where you cannot maintain them. Now that is just me, but could that message also be the one conveyed to your guests?

Over the past several years, we have become acutely aware of the essence of "story." We hear this term used in the church world and in business settings. It has been used to prompt people to open up about their lives and life experiences-to tell their story. On a "corporate" level, it is the interwoven thread used to identify the mission, vision, direction, and passion of organizations. The reality is, we all have a story. Some of these stories are sensational, while others may seem mundane or routine. Others grip our emotions and pull on our heartstrings while transforming us into the story.

What has grasped me lately is that everyone and everything has a story to tell and that people are "reading" those stories even when we are not aware. We do not have to write a screenplay or book to tell our story. When we walk into a room full of people, you will start to read certain aspects of people's stories, and they will begin to read yours as well. They might not see the entire story, but they will see some pretty apparent chapters in that story. The way you enter the room will tell the chapter of your story related to your self-confidence or possibly your physical attributes or limitations. The way you greet other guests will convey yet another part of the story, as will the clothes you are wearing. In addition, the room itself tells a story (more on that later).

The concept of "storytelling" has become an "Ah-ha" moment for me. I have learned that some of the most interesting, complex, intuitive, and compelling parts of my story are those where they are observed and not heard. If I have to verbally communicate that a component of my story is generosity and kindness, then it is very likely that those attributes are not part of my non-fiction story, but rather a fictional trait that I want people to believe about me. Conversely, congruent stories are generally seen and felt long before anyone tells them out loud. I think that some parts of our story, those with the most intrinsic value, are never spoken. We did not need to hear Mother Theresa tell us she loved orphans. We do not need to listen to a speech by Shaquille O'Neil to know that he is a large man who has done well for himself as a professional athlete. We do not need a mother, rocking her baby, to tell us that she loves that little gift from God. No, we can see it. We can feel it. There is something that communicates the story to us just by looking at the person or the situation.

"Story" is all around us. It is in virtually every aspect of our daily experiences, which means that our church and ministry facilities also tell a story. The questions for church leaders are:

What story are your facilities/campus telling?

Are we intentional about the story?

Is the story congruent with who we are, who we "think we are," what we believe/value, and who we want to reach for Christ?

As a final thought — and one that might feel contrived — let me challenge your thinking about the origin of the facility management profession. The original facility managers were considered holy men. Take a few minutes to read Numbers 3:14-38.

I had never seen this before, but when I did, it jumped off the page and hit me like a ton of bricks.

God set the Levites apart and designated them as the first church facility managers. God personally assigned, consecrated, and wrote the job description for the first facility managers for his house of worship. This is not just a play on words or me taking scripture out of context; this is real.

Pay close attention to these verses:

25 These two clans were responsible to care for the Tabernacle, including the sacred tent with its layers of coverings, the curtain at its entrance, 26 the curtains of the courtyard that surrounded the Tabernacle and altar, the curtain at the courtyard entrance, the ropes, and all the equipment related to their use. (NLT)

And further down...

31 These four clans were responsible for the care of the Ark, the table, the lampstand, the altars, the various articles used in the sanctuary, the inner curtain, and all the equipment related to their use. 32 Eleazar, son of Aaron the priest, was the chief administrator over all the Levites, with special responsibility for the oversight of the sanctuary. (NLT)

Finally...

35 They were assigned the area north of the Tabernacle for their camp. The leader of the Merarite clans was Zuriel son of Abihail. 36 These two clans were responsible for the care of the frames supporting the Tabernacle, the crossbars, the pillars, the bases, and all the equipment related to their use. (NLT)

Don't miss this! Not only were the Levite clans, as a whole, assigned these tasks, but God assigned leaders for each clan to oversee the performance of these holy duties. Sounds a lot like a facility manager's role.

Re-read verse 32.

Eleazar, son of Aaron the priest, was the chief administrator over all the Levites, with special responsibility for the oversight of the sanctuary. Not only did the clans have overseers, there was a Chief Administrator (NIV = Chief Leader, KJV = Chief over the Chief of Levites). Whatever translation or version you want to reference, the point is obvious: someone needed to be in charge of the overall well-being of the sanctuary, and that position was an elevated position in the eyes of God and the nation of Israel. This role was important enough that God personally set the ground rules for it and assigned the person he thought best to address it. He did not instruct Moses to select slaves or the foreigners living with them. Instead, he picked the cream of the crop! The son of the High Priest was hand-selected to be "the man."

Where in the scripture does it give such vivid instruction and place such honor on a role in the church for, say, the youth pastor? Singles pastor? Small groups pastor?

I can hear it now: *But Tim, those are ministers of the gospel. They are referenced all throughout scripture. You are taking this out of context. The "church" is the people, not the meeting place.* I can hear others saying: *But we are not under the law, like Moses and Aaron.* And for many of these arguments, I would agree. I would never place the importance of people's souls, lives, and relationships above the designing, building, or caring for any facility. I would never want to forego the gift of God's grace for a set of rules.

But, to use an old adage, have we become so heavenly-minded that we are of no earthly good? Have we so elevated other roles that the role of those who have been entrusted to steward what God has given us is at the bottom of the organizational chart? Please consider this as you make decisions about the facility manager role and as you interact with your facility manager.

CHAPTER 13
THE FACILITY MANAGEMENT TEAM

As I mentioned earlier, properly stewarding the facilities entrusted to you isn't a one-person job…it requires a team. This team might consist entirely of paid staff members, all volunteers, vendors and suppliers, or a mixture of each. However that needs to work at your church, there's one question I get all the time…

How many facility staff do we need?

I have heard this more the past couple of years than ever before. As church leaders explore how to steward the tools God has entrusted to them, they realize the necessary tasks and functions related to such care occurs through qualified people.

We refer to our church facilities as the "House of God." However, it is not a house. It is a complex commercial facility. And while I wholeheartedly believe God could miraculously fix the HVAC system or stop a roof leak, I do not think He wants us to use that as our facility management strategy. Let's remember God is the one that created the laws of nature, which include aging, wear/tear, life cycles, deterioration, rot, etc. So, it is incumbent on us to address our facility issues, and that takes people.

I've tried to find a data-driven source for a nice and neat rule of thumb for how many Full-Time Equivalents (FTEs) are necessary to keep a facility looking and operating at peak condition. Unfortunately, such research was not readily available for the church market, *sigh!*

In light of that, I conducted a research project with about 100 church facilities across the country, which included a variety of campus sizes, construction types, age, philosophy, and the like. On average, my survey indicated that 1 FTE per 25,000 - 30,000 square feet was typical.

Some of the churches I surveyed with larger facilities have a much denser FTE to square foot ratio, as many have facility staff to do in-house repairs and servicing on the HVAC and other systems. The number of FTEs would be impacted if outsourcing these activities were implemented.

There are other factors not fully vetted in the survey, such as:

- Setup crew responsibilities
- Crossover of Housekeeping/Janitorial with setup and/or other general maintenance
- Grounds maintenance responsibilities

Even with some facilities being grossly underserved and others with extensive staff, it appears 25,000 - 30,000 square feet per FTE is the prudent number to be shooting for, PLUS your managerial staff and janitorial staff.

This may be a tough pill to swallow, and I am sure many are shocked. Regardless, it would be wise to start to review your facility staffing and to plan for the future accordingly. You will be glad you did. I am also a realist, and there are always variations to this, such as, if you outsource all your maintenance, you may need fewer people per square foot. Or, if you have 35,000 square feet, you may still be able to properly manage the facility with just one FTE.

Now that we've addressed how many people you'll need on your church's facility management team, let's discuss the roles you need to fill.

Depending on the size of your facility and the staffing model you decide to employ (the combination of staff, volunteers, and contractors), here's a list of potential roles to fill:

- Facility Manager
- Assistant Facility Manager
- Custodian
- Facilities Setup Coordinator
- Facilities Crew Leader
- Maintenance Technician
- Groundskeeper
- Security
- Food Service Director
- Cook
- Kitchen Assistant

To download sample job descriptions for these roles, go to http://www.smartchurchsolutions.com/entrustedresources.

CHAPTER 14
SHOULD WE OUTSOURCE?

Sometimes hiring full-time or even part-time staff to clean, perform maintenance, and handle other facility-related tasks isn't the best use of church finances. Bringing in a company to manage those tasks might be the most cost-effective way to get the job done with excellence.

Here are a few items to consider when deciding whether to use an outsourcer:

Item #1: Candidate Availability

Do you have a difficult time finding qualified candidates to perform the maintenance or janitorial tasks needed to steward your facilities properly? If so, finding an outsourcing vendor might be an easier option as they'll have scoured the labor pool for the right people.

Item #2: Oversight

One myth about outsourcing is that you don't have to invest the time to manage or oversee an outsourcer. That's not the case. You'll still need to monitor their work. However, a quality outsourcing vendor will have clearly defined performance metrics which you'll agree upon from the start. The vendor should provide you with those metrics regularly (weekly, monthly, etc.). They should also submit reports on maintenance activities, so you have that well-documented. As you can see, one of the benefits of outsourcing is that the vendor provides the metrics you need, thus removing the responsibility of defining and updating them yourself.

Item #3: Qualifications

What should we look for in an outsourcing company?

- Do they conduct background checks on their employees and provide you with proof that each person who will be on church property passed the background check?
- Before providing you with a quote for services, will the vendor visit your facilities to get a complete understanding of what you'll need them to handle?
- Does the vendor provide you with a formal contract including information on their insurance coverage, background checks of their employees, their fees, when payment is due and by what method, how often they'll perform each service, etc.?
- Are they able to provide references - specifically from other churches they work for?
- Do they provide a single individual who manages the relationship with your church?
- Talk with them about what cleaning products they will use, how to confirm those are what they're using on your facilities, etc.

Once you obtain quotes from a few vendors, compare that to what it would cost to hire staff to perform those services. Don't forget to include a fully loaded set of costs for an employee, such as health insurance, paid time off, etc. Add in costs for the cleaning products and supplies you'll need to have on-hand if you perform these tasks in-house. Also, consider the time you'll spend training staff members. Weigh the costs and consider the pros/cons of either approach before making a final decision.

Chapter 15
Facility Management Software

Regardless of who performs the work, you still need to track what tasks are outstanding, who's assigned to each, when each assignment is due, and much more.

So, how do you track and process work requests at your facility?

- Legal Pad?
- Excel spreadsheet?
- Post-it Notes?
- Cross your fingers, then hope and pray?

Even the best facility management team in the world would have a tough time keeping track of all tasks without a central system. Let's explore some available options for tracking work orders, service history, equipment inventory and condition, capital improvements, defective equipment log, vendor log, on-site maintenance staff assignments, and so much more. We will investigate the needs of most churches to track service requests and work orders, as well as being proactive in monitoring capital improvements to assist in your annual budgeting process.

To get started, let's develop some common language. Here are some words and phrases that will help us in this discussion:

1. **Service Request:** A request from within your church/ministry (i.e., It is too hot in our classroom, the copier is not working, the toilet is clogged, etc. *Sound familiar?*).

2. **Work Order Process:** The system/process used to facilitate the inspection, review, accept, and fulfill the service request.

3. **Scheduled Maintenance:** Items that reoccur regularly (or should occur regularly). These can include preventive maintenance items (i.e., HVAC servicing, changing filters, systematic replacement of light bulbs, certification of fire extinguishers, regular maintenance on elevators and other systems with moving parts) as well as other items that need to be scheduled and tracked on a regular basis (i.e., housekeeping items, yard maintenance, mulch in the plant beds, window cleaning, carpet cleaning, etc.).

4. **Capital Improvement Needs:** These are items identified as having a predicted life cycle with a predetermined or expected end of useful life/service. These items would require capital funds to replace or significantly modify to extend or start a new life cycle (i.e., replacement of HVAC equipment, paving the parking lot, replacing or recoating roofing materials, replacement of floor coverings, etc.).

5. **Vendor Management:** Who works on your facility? Is it on-staff personnel, outside vendors, volunteers, or a combination of these options? Regardless of who does the work, you need to assign the work and then follow up on the completion of the work. You also need to track Certificates of Insurance for vendors that are not on staff at the church. There needs to be clear and definitive communication to all personnel performing services for the church including assigning of work, tracking of the work, issuing the proper paperwork (i.e., work orders, PO's, work scopes, "not to exceed" amounts for the work, warranty fulfillment, and so much more). All of this would fall under the category of Vendor Management.

6. **Asset/Inventory Management and Tracking:** Your facility has HVAC equipment, light fixtures, bulbs, plumbing fixtures, water heaters, kitchen equipment, IT equipment, office equipment, yard equipment, cleaning

equipment, and the list goes on. What is your process for tracking the manufacturer, make, model, components, warranty remaining, quantity of items, service history (the last time the equipment was serviced, repaired or replaced), and other aspects associated with this equipment? Do you currently have a system or process to schedule work orders and preventive maintenance for each specific item? Do you know the make and model number of all of your equipment? If not, why not?

Now that we have a common language, let's consider how you can develop a process and system to help you with managing your facilities. To keep this all in perspective, let's not forget our ministry facilities are large complex commercial structures, with several costly moving parts that need to be maintained, serviced, and repaired.

Why should your church consider using some form of work order management software or Facility Management software (Also referred to as a CMMS - Computerized Maintenance Management System)? Isn't that just for big churches with big facilities and big budgets and big staff?

As I've mentioned previously, our church facilities are large complex commercial structures. Even if your facility is less than 10,000 square feet, it is a commercial structure and it is complex. It may be the "house of God," but it ain't no house.

Regardless of the size of your facility, take a minute to answer the following questions:

1.   Does your facility have more than one HVAC unit? If so, do you have more than five "tons" of cooling/heating capacity?

2.   Does your facility have an electrical service that is larger than 400 amps?

3.   Do you have paved parking spaces with a curb cut to a city, town, county, state, or federal road?

4. Do you have an automatic fire sprinkler system?

5. Do you have a fire alarm system?

6. Do you have exit signs and emergency lights?

7. Do you have ceilings higher than ten feet with light fixtures in those ceilings?

8. Is any part of your roof over 30 feet tall?

9. Do you have more than one water heater?

10. Is any part of your building made of steel/metal?

If you answered yes to two or more of the above questions, then you likely have a complex commercial structure. With that type of structure is the need for scheduled maintenance, repairs, and service. In most cases, these tasks exceed the ability of the typical "residential" handyman. They need to be completed by skilled professionals in these trades, whether from inside your congregation or not.

I can hear you saying, *"Okay, we agree with you in principle, but so what?"* Good question. Well, let me start with the nine most obvious reasons why you should be using Facility Management software.

Reason #1: Be INTENTIONAL

There is a quote that most of you have heard before, but I believe is so appropriate for this discussion.

"If you fail to plan, you are planning to fail! - Benjamin Franklin[1]

We do not plan to forget to change the HVAC filters or to clean the coils or to clean the carpet. However, without a plan, these things become lost in the hustle and bustle of the "urgent" items that absorb our daily activities. When that happens, the low-cost maintenance items become higher cost repair issues. Having a proactive system that will serve as your "reminder" for these items will not only save you time but assist you in being intentional with the care and maintenance of your facility. Remember, these facilities were entrusted to our care.

Reason #2: Central Database/Repository

Do you have a spreadsheet here, a post-it note there, an email requesting work be done, a legal pad full of ideas, and your computer calendar set with dozens of reminders? Unfortunately, this is more the norm than the exception. We met with a new client who said, "When all four of us involved in the care of our facility are together, we then have all the needed data." So, what happens when only two of them are together? Do they only have 50% of the needed data and information? We hear this over and over again from churches of all sizes.

Having a single source to input and store your facility data is critical. You need to have a single secure place to store data, process work orders, track historical data, evaluate work requests, and manage vendors. And, it needs to be accessible to all the key players and stakeholders at the church. Without this single repository, you will always be subject to missing critical data when you need it most.

Reason #3: Risk Management

What would happen to all of your data, plans, procedures, systems, processes, etc., if the key person at your church is, heaven forbid, hit by a truck? Would you lose all the data that is squirreled away in their head? Would you find yourself starting from scratch? What things might go undone or undetected until something major broke-down? Would you know where all of the files were stored and what vendors had contracts with the church or what promises had been made? I have met dozens of great facility managers. They know their facilities like the back of their hands, and they are invaluable to their church. But what if suddenly they were gone? Would you be prepared?

Reason #4: Long-Term Capital Improvement Planning

I have been surprised by how many churches do not have an active "sinking fund" or some form of capital improvements process. When we ask them about their planning process for major capital expenses (i.e., replacing flooring, replacing HVAC equipment, resurfacing parking, etc.), the much too common answer is, "We wait until it breaks and then replace it." OUCH! This does not sound like planning. It's funny that we do such a tremendous job when we plan for a building expansion or new construction project. We set aside money in a building fund, evaluate the costs, and plan accordingly. However, it is more common than not that this level of proactive planning dies when a church moves into the building. Having a proactive plan means to project and plan for future capital expenditures.

Reason #5: Work Prioritization

Does the "urgent" take precedence over the important? Does that last email or call take you off task? Ever walk into the office and know you have a million things to do but don't know where to start? Do you feel like you have a mountain of work: emails, projects, emergencies? Well, you are not alone. Frankly, I feel exactly like that as I am typing this. I have a fence to repair, bills to pay, accounting to update, and so much more. The use of software solutions can be a tremendous asset to staying on point and keeping work prioritized. If it were not for Outlook, I would forget where I am supposed to be, everyone's phone numbers, and even when to take certain meds (I know, I am a mess). If it were not for my Salesforce.com account, I would not be able to stay on task with the people I need to follow up with or to get a proposal out. Facility Management software can do the same thing for your facility team. It can set the priority of the work, set an ETA for the work to be complete, and send email alerts and reminders. Trying to keep all of this in your head or on a legal pad will only increase the stock value for pain relievers.

Reason #6: Vendor Management

Who is approved to work on your site? How do you track their names, address, emails, phone numbers, etc.? How do you dispatch work to the vendors? Fax? Phone? Morse Code? Most good Facility Management software solutions will, at the very least, provide a section to list all of the pertinent data about your vendors and subcontractors. This is a necessity.

The better systems will also provide a means for assigning work orders to vendors and dispatch the work orders via an automated system through email, text messages, or some similar method. The very best we have seen will also allow you to do an "end of work" evaluation of the work that will create a historical thread of data for your future reference. We believe these tools are vital to the success of your workflow and will save you a great deal of time and frustration in the future.

Reason #7: Historical Data

I've used the P90X workout series, and the trainer keeps saying to write down what weights we use and how many reps. He uses a little phrase to say, "If you don't know what you've done, how can you know what you need to do?" That same thinking applies to our building management and maintenance. If you don't track what you have done, then how do you know what work to complete in the future? If you neglect to document when an HVAC unit was last serviced, how will you know when it's due for additional maintenance? Having a database that lists your equipment and the historical data will give you great insight into the condition of the equipment and the steps that may need to be taken in the future. This kind of tracking is not just to have data of the past, but also to help plan for the future.

Reason #8: Asset Database

- Do you know the make, model, serial number, and filter size of each piece of equipment at your facility?
- Do you know what kind of light bulbs you have and how many fixtures in the facility use that type of bulb?
- What size of water heaters do you have? What's the make and model number of each?
- How many exit signs do you have, and what kind of bulbs do they utilize?

Now, I would not expect you to know all of this off the top of your head, but could you, with a few clicks, get to this data? Is it written on a legal pad or tucked away in the corner of your mind? We already addressed the potential issues with these applications. These are tough questions that need to be asked and answered.

Reason #9: Warranty Tracking

Have you ever paid for a service call to later find out that it was under warranty? How did that make you feel? Were you able to get a full refund? I have witnessed, far too often, cases when a church has work done because something is not functioning correctly without much consideration to the warranty that was still active. This is a waste of Kingdom dollars, and, quite frankly, it frustrates me. I've had clients calling subcontractors to get work done, and in some cases paying directly for said work, when the work was the responsibility of the general contractor that built the space. This was not the contractor's fault, but rather the church did not have a system in place to know what items were still under warranty. They spent money unnecessarily, and wasted time chasing things down. (How do you put a price on that?) Knowing warranty coverage for your major components can save you a great deal of money, short and long-term.

This wraps up the "why" portion, next, we will look at the features you should consider when evaluating different solutions. And yes, I suggest you do your due diligence to find the right solution for your church. There are several good applications on the market. Some are geared primarily toward churches, while others offer more "commercial" applications but may still meet your needs. Do your research and take advantage of free web demos as they can be invaluable.

What are the features you should consider?

Minimum Features:

- Produce and Assess Work Orders and requested repairs. We believe your system should allow your staff/personnel to notify you of the need for service. The service request should provide enough information to the recipient to assess the issue before they physically explore it further.

- Prioritize the Requests. As part of the service request process, the sender should be able to establish a "priority" of the service request, at least in their minds. This will give the recipient a heads-up as to how the sender perceives this issue.

- Track Work Orders. Most of the better products on the market allow you to track the full life cycle of a work order.

- Historical Data. This is very important. What is the historical data associated with your equipment? When was the last time it was serviced and what were the issues at that time? If the system does not track this, then you will have to do it manually, which would be redundant.

- Upgraded Features:

- <u>Track Vendors and Assign Work Orders directly to them (even if in-house or volunteers).</u> The better systems on the market will provide for the tracking of the subcontractors, suppliers, and vendors associated with the care of your facilities. Who are they? What service categories do they work in? How do I reach them? Who is my primary contact? Are they a volunteer group in the church? In addition, the ability to have an automated process for sending work orders can save you valuable time and money, not to mention a reduction in misunderstandings.

- <u>Email Notification Process for All Work.</u> The best systems on the market have an automated notification process. These should include notifications for when a service request is issued, when an ETA is established by the vendor, when the work is complete, and if the work is going to exceed the agreed to projected cost. As it is said, time is money, and these systems are meant to save time.

- <u>Asset Tracking and Assigning of Work Orders to Specific Equipment.</u> Ideally, you should be able to track all the equipment in your facility. It is best if you can catalog all of your equipment and then be able to tie a work order to a specific piece of equipment. If you cannot catalog the equipment and track it, then it may not be the right product for you.

- <u>Assessment tools</u> such as life cycle projections, energy usage, defective equipment tracking, capital improvement tracking and projections. How are you currently projecting the life cycle cost of your equipment? Do you have an ongoing list of capital improvements that need to be made? How do you track your utility costs? Having the ability to track these items in one centralized place will make the long-term management of your facilities more effective.

Again, I recommend you research a variety of tools to determine which will be the best fit for your church. However, I would be remiss (and a crummy CEO) if I didn't suggest you check out the tool we've created at Smart Church Solutions called eSPACE. You can get the full run-down over at www.smartchurchsolutions.com/espace/work-order-management. Don't just take my word for it that it's an amazing tool (although it is).

Here's what some of our customers have to say about it:

"We have been using eSPACE with COOLSPACE for three years, and our church saw a 30% reduction in utility expense immediately after installation. The interface is easy to manage, easy to teach to our staff, and we can make adjustments from anywhere. COOLSPACE has now paid for itself several times over in return on investment as we've saved on electric bills and maintenance. No more lock-boxes on thermostats, and no more forgetting to "turn the air up on the way out" after a service or event." - Hank Garner, First Baptist Church of Columbia

"I have been managing our church facility for nearly 14 years and while I have experimented with other software tools to help me, Cool Solutions Group is hands down the best out there. Cost savings, better stewardship and higher production of our church's support staff are a direct result of their Event, Work Order and HVAC management software. The relationship our church has with Smart Church Solutions is built on trust because we know they will always be there to support our mission and will continually innovate to do that." - Luke Littrell, Fellowship Bible Church

"Using eSPACE scheduling software has reduced staff time by 25% when it comes to scheduling rooms and HVAC. Before eSPACE, staff was entering the event into the calendar program to reserve the space and then entering the event into the HVAC control program to control temperature. We were always getting frantic calls about "the HVAC is not on" when we forgot. Sometimes we would heat or cool a complete building for long periods of time, while it was not occupied, to ensure the HVAC was on when it needed to be. When you enter an event into eSPACE not only is the space reserved but the HVAC is taken care of and out of mind. Staff is now able to spend more time on ministry and less time worrying about HVAC." - Jeff McClanahan, Living Hope Baptist

"Using eSPACE scheduling software has reduced staff time by 25% when it comes to scheduling rooms and HVAC. Before eSPACE, staff was entering the event into the calendar program to reserve the space and then entering the event into the HVAC control program to control temperature. We were always getting frantic calls about the HVAC is not on when we forgot. Sometimes we would heat or cool a complete building for long periods of time, while it was not occupied, to ensure the HVAC was on when it needed to be. When you enter an event into eSPACE not only is the space reserved but the HVAC is taken care of and out of mind. Staff is now able to spend more time on ministry and less time worrying about HVAC." - Marlin Yoder, Church Administrator

Section 4: Budgeting - Preparing Financially for the Inevitable

We've addressed the details of day-to-day facility stewardship, staffing, and potential automation options through facility management software. So, how do you pay for all this? Excellent question! That's what we'll explore next as we move into the financial aspects of facility stewardship. No, you probably didn't get into ministry with a burning desire to crunch numbers and discuss budgets. However, properly stewarding the facilities God has entrusted to you requires money. The key to handling facility-related finances wisely (and any budget, for that matter) is to plan ahead and set aside cash for inevitable expenses.

CHAPTER 16
3 INITIAL BUCKETS FOR FACILITY BUDGETING

With this in mind, one question I often receive from ministry leaders is, *"How do we develop an intentional facility budget? How will we know we have enough now and in the future? Our buildings are not getting any younger!"*

I hear that a lot from Pastors, Executive Pastors, Business Administrators, Facility Managers, and laypeople. It is a universal concern. When you take into account that there are roughly 350,000 churches in America that all meet in a facility and the majority of those facilities are either owned by the church or they are long term leases, then you can see why this is such a critical issue. While facilities will NEVER save a soul, they are an incredibly important component of our church life. To top it off, a facility is generally in the top 2-3 largest line items in any church budget. This is important stuff!

Let's take a look from 30,000 feet to view the most effective means by which we have seen work. This will not be exhaustive but will give you an incredible framework in developing your facility/operational budget.

When you are budgeting for your facilities, there are three primary buckets you need to consider. (Well, really there are four, but we'll address the fourth one in the next chapter.) Let's look at each one:

Bucket #1: Operational

This includes utilities, janitorial, general maintenance, and staffing. Budgeting these areas will be critical to get right. What does that mean? It means ensuring you are not spending too much on utilities and making sure you are spending enough in the other areas to keep up with the natural rate of deterioration. Remember: All facilities deteriorate at a rate of approximately 2.5% per year. Keeping pace with that requires planning and dollars.

Here are some rules of thumb that we find to represent "best-practices" for churches:

Utilities:

A reasonable range here is about $1.00-1.50/square foot annually. If your utility costs are over $1.25/square foot, you may want to consider an energy audit or a review of your HVAC controls, as 50% or more of your energy consumption is attributed to HVAC. The best way to reduce that is through proper "behavior," which you can assist with proper controls. What do I mean by behavior? Great question. Think of it like this...do you turn your HVAC systems on first thing in the morning then let them run all day without consideration of the actual facility use? That is "behavior" driven usage...not intentional. Or, think of this from Colby May of LIT Consulting – "Every degree that we adjust on our thermostat equips the HVAC portion of our utility bill by 1.5%. So an average cooling temperature of 72° verses 65° can save up to 10.5%." Those are prime examples of how changing behavior can change our energy consumption.

Janitorial:

This category includes expenses related to labor, material, paper products, major cleaning like carpet extractions, window cleaning, etc.) and should be in the $1.50-$2.50 range annually.

General Maintenance:

If this is below the national average of $2.25 – $3.00/square foot, then this should be re-evaluated. We have found that if general maintenance is underfunded, the likelihood of deferred maintenance increases. The premise is that if you don't account sufficiently for general maintenance to care for the natural rate of facility deterioration, you will "defer" those costs. I'll address this more below.

Staff:

Based on national surveys by our firm and IFMA, we believe the number of facility staff for a well-run organization is one Full Time Facility Staff Employee for every 25,000 – 35,000 square feet. This is not for cleaning...that is another story...this is for general maintenance.

Bucket #2: Deferred Maintenance

As I mentioned earlier, these are the items that should have been addressed previously but, for whatever reason, have not been accounted for. We have found that when insufficient general maintenance is budgeted, the likelihood of deferred maintenance increases...same for staffing.

I read a blog that quoted Rick Biedenweg, President of Pacific Partners Consulting Group and former Assistant Vice President of information resources at Stanford University. In that blog, Mr. Biedenweg said:

"Every $1 in deferred maintenance costs $4 of capital renewal needs in the future."[1]

WOW...that is a kick in the gut. I have taught for years that if we do not keep up with the natural rate of deterioration (1-4% of the current replacement value – CRV) that the rate can more than double. This reinforces this premise as the compounding factor of not spending $1 today, can grow four-fold as the deterioration continues...coupled with the future value of time and money.

While Biedenweg worked primarily with the educational system and their needs, we can use his numbers and research with any type of maintenance department. Their research indicates educational institutions should be spending 0.5% (annually) of their building and system's current replacement value on ongoing maintenance and regular preventive maintenance and 1.5% of CRV on capital repairs. Again, this solidifies and accentuates the positions we have taken related to Facility Stewardship and the need for intentional and proactive long term planning.

Consider the following quote from an article called *Geaslin's Inverse-Square Rule for Deferred Maintenance Effort*© by David Tod Geaslin. This made my head hurt!

"If a part is known to be failing but operated to failure (OTF), the resultant energy required to overcome the breakdown event to the entire organization will be the square of the cost of the primary failure part. If the breakdown event escalates, the energy required to recover from the breakdown will continue to square at each successive level of failure."[2]

So...what is the bright side of this? It is never too late to get started to turn the tide. That work begins by allocating money in the budget to deal with deferred maintenance and get caught up ASAP.

Bucket #3: Capital Projects

These would be the type of projects that may include adding space or major renovations, expansions, and the like. It would be "easy" to see the need for some added space and be tempted to take the money from one of the above buckets. Be VERY careful with that thinking...that is a slippery slope. Also, small projects like painting, replacing a few light fixtures, etc. could, and should, be part of your General Maintenance budget.

Being intentional about each bucket will keep you out of the dog house related to your facilities. If we were proactive with our operational budgets and capital reserves, there would not be any deferred maintenance.

In a perfect world, we would properly fund our general maintenance budget to keep the building in the best physical condition possible. We would also have adequate capital reserves so that when we approach the "end of life" of our facility components there would not be deferred maintenance.

CHAPTER 17

FACILITY RETIREMENT PLANNING

(Or...How to make sure the church's A/C works in the middle of a Texas summer.)

Once you've developed budgets for facility operations, deferred maintenance, and capital projects, the next item to consider is retirement. We all know we need to plan for retirement. We set up retirement accounts, take advantage of tax-free plans, and determine how much we'll need to live comfortably once we retire. Well, that's what we're supposed to do anyway.

However, have you ever considered the fact that each aspect of your church facility will, at some point, need to retire? That HVAC system you've had for ten years will retire itself in a few years (whether you're ready or not)- the same thing with flooring, lighting fixtures, windows, pavement, and more. To be prepared for the retirement of these items, you'll need a fully funded capital reserve account.

Capital reserve planning is one of the most overlooked aspects of facility ownership. Most organizations have no trouble raising or borrowing funds to build their facilities and budget for the daily operational expenses. Unfortunately, many (may I say "most") forget that their buildings are constructed with systems and materials that are all deteriorating. As such, you'll have to replace nearly every component of the facility at some point - and the rate of deterioration will vary based on a whole host of variables.

A great deal of our work has been with institutional organizations (houses of worship, churches, schools, colleges, etc.). Many have been not-for-profit, and, unfortunately, are some of the worst culprits in the neglect of long-term capital repair and reserve planning. They are not alone. Many other market sectors suffer from the same "disease."

So what should you do? What is a capital reserve account? Is it different from a "sinking fund"? Is it different from a contingency fund or excess annual budget?

Capital Reserve: A type of account of an organization that is reserved for long-term capital investment projects or any other large and anticipated expense(s) that will be incurred in the future. This type of reserve fund is set aside to ensure that the organization has adequate funding to at least partially finance the project.

A simplified definition is...Capital Reserve: "an amount of money that a company or organization keeps in a special account for future needs."[3]

Did you catch the three key words in that definition?

1. MONEY - This is cash. This is NOT the promise of cash. It is NOT an IOU. It is cold, hard CASH!

2. SPECIAL ACCOUNT - It is NOT a slush fund. It is NOT excess balance in the budget. It is NOT commingled dollars. It is set aside specifically for this purpose.

3. FUTURE - This money is not for the immediate. It is for the future, somewhere down the road.

In short, a capital reserve account is one that is established to save up money, in a designated account, to pay for a major capital expenditure (replacement, repurposing, etc.) when its effective life is over. For example, the average life of your HVAC systems may be 15 years. If you spend $100,000 on a new HVAC system today, how much should you set aside in a reserve account to have the adequate funds to replace it in 15 years? Is it $100,000? More? Less?

To prepare for a fully-funded capital reserve account, you must take these intentional steps:

Step #1: Address Deferred Maintenance

If you have any deferred maintenance, you must develop a plan to bring things up to "snuff" based on their age and expected life. If that is not done before developing the ongoing Capital Reserves, you will always be playing catch up.

Step #2: Research Current Replacement Value (CRV)

What would it cost today to replace the item?

Step #3: Estimate the Expected "Life"

How many years of life should we still expect from this item?

Step #4: Determine Annual Inflation

As you look at the economic environment, what percentage of annual inflation would be prudent to plan on?

Step #5: Develop an Annual Budget

Based on the above, how much money should we set aside every year?

By addressing these five simple items, you can project the total replacement cost and the annual amount to set aside. Now, you are smart enough to know that this simplistic approach is not 100% foolproof, but it will get you close, and my guess it will get you a LOT closer than what you are currently allocating. Of course, there will be times when the percentage of inflation is off or the years of life are misjudged.

Regardless, you will have set aside money to help you cover the cost instead of having to do a capital campaign just to replace the carpet or buy new HVAC units.

So, how do you get started?

Start by prioritizing which items you'll eventually need to replace based on these categories:

Category #1: Largest Line Items

- HVAC
- Roofing
- Asphalt/Paving
- Floor Covering

Category #2: Operational Impact

- HVAC (see a pattern)
- Building Envelope (Windows, Caulk, Doors, Insulation, Air/Water Intrusion)
- Lighting/Electrical
- Roofing (think about how a leaky roof impacts operation)

Category #3: Visual Impact

- Parking and site concrete
- Floor finishes
- Wall Finishes
- Lighting

From there, take a look at the Life Cycle Calculator (https://www.smartchurchsolutions.com/espace/lifecycle-calculator) developed by the team at Smart Church Solutions and eSPACE. This tool is an inexpensive (it is actually FREE) way to:

1. Track physical assets

2. Set Current Replacement Values (CRV)

3. Project inflation impacts

4.   Set budget amounts on an annual basis for all items and assets

5.   See a dashboard of dollars needed each year

6.   Set reminders and alerts for key milestone dates related to the replacement of these items

7.   Track depreciable assets and track the annual depreciation of the same

8.   Interface with the eSPACE Work Order Management application to further increase efficiency and effectiveness.

By investing in a capital reserve account, you're making it easier and less stressful to replace vital components of the church facility. When you must repave the parking lot or replace the HVAC (not if, but when), you'll have the money readily available to handle those purchases. That's good stewardship of church finances and facilities of what has been entrusted to us.

Section 5: Facility Assessment - Time to Face Reality

O kay, we've covered A LOT of ground here. You might be feeling a bit overwhelmed and wondering what to do with this information. Don't worry, I've got you covered. As the old saying goes, "Every journey begins with a single step."

Here's the first step I recommend you take: Assess your church facilities.

After all, you don't know the full scope of what you need to do until you've evaluated the current state of your facilities.

My team at Smart Church Solutions performs what we call, "Facility Condition Assessments" for churches all the time all across the country. We have a standard list of things we want to look at and evaluate as we walk the facility. As we identify areas that are showing disrepair or that need attention, we note those for our clients. That's what I recommend you do for your facilities (unless you want to hire us to do it, then that's okay too!).

This activity requires you to look at your facilities with a fresh, critical eye. It's easy to overlook a few scuffs on the wall, a cracked tile, or dust on the ceiling fan in your home when you're there every day. However, if you have guests over for dinner, they won't be able to help but see some of these issues. They have the advantage of having "fresh eyes" when they walk in the door. Your familiarity with your church facilities is something to overcome as you perform this facility assessment.

CHAPTER 18

CONDUCT A FACILITY CONDITION ASSESSMENT

What should you inspect as you conduct this assessment? Here's a list of items to get you started:

Let's begin with a pre-assessment evaluation:

1. What is the life expectancy of the roof(s) at your facility?

2. How many more years will your HVAC systems last and how much will they cost to replace?

3. Do you have any mold, asbestos, or other environmental issues?

4. What kind of "First Impression" will your facilities have on a guest?

5. How do your operational costs compare to industry benchmarks?

6. Are your facilities safe?

7. Do your facilities meet code(s)?

8. Do you have any "Life Safety" issues that could be a hazard to your members and guests?

9. Is your property still insurable for its replacement value?

10. Are your facilities as energy efficient as possible, and are you keeping up with the changes in technology and laws?

If you're unable to answer these questions quickly or if you answered them in the negative, it's time to take a hard look at your facility stewardship program. You may have known that intuitively and that's why you bought this book. That's a great place to start!

Next, here are areas to evaluate as you walk through your facility:

#1: Parking Lot

Take a close look at the condition of the asphalt, whether parking space stripes are easily visible or have faded, and if parking space bumpers are in good condition. Check all lights to ensure they're functioning properly. Evaluate parking lot signage, including handicapped signs, consider the general accessibility (or lack thereof) of the lot, and check the curbs, gutters, and any potential drainage issues.

#2: Landscaping

How does the lawn look? Is the grass green in the warmer months, or do you have several areas of dead grass to patch? When was the last time someone trimmed the scrubs? Do you have overgrown trees or bushes that a "bad guy" could hide behind? Are the beds well-mulched and have healthy plants or flowers growing in them?

Check out any irrigation systems you have in place and consider whether any detention/retention ponds are working effectively. Take a good look at all sidewalks, ramps, and stairs to see if any cracks or chips need to be repaired.

Finally, inspect any fencing around the property. Check for any holes, paint or stain that may need to be redone, etc.

#3: Roofing Elements

Inspect the roof for potential leaks or displaced shingles/materials. Check all gutters, scuppers, and drains. Don't forget any awnings, canopies, steeples, cupolas, or towers - you need to look carefully at each to see if they require any maintenance or repairs.

#4: Exterior Cladding

Look at the outside of each building. Are there any cracks in the brick or stucco? Does any of the siding need to be replaced or repainted? Could the exterior walls use a good power-washing?

#5: Doors and Windows

Do any of the doors need to be repainted? Do all of them function properly? Do any of the doors squeak or sound like you're about to enter a haunted house when you open them? Hint: a few squirts of WD-40 can quickly expel any "ghosts."

Are the windows clean? Do you see any cracks in the caulking around the windows? Does each window open easily? From the inside, do the window coverings (blinds, shutters, or curtains) look to be in good condition?

#6: Flooring

Moving indoors, look down as you move through the building. Do you see any cracks in tiles or in the tile grout? Are the floor mats clean and in good condition? Look for stains or rips in the carpet or on vinyl flooring.

#7: Interior Walls

Look closely at each wall. Are there scuff marks, cracks, chipped paint, water stains, or other signs of disrepair on the walls? Is any wallpaper torn or faded?

How about the ceiling? Do you have stained ceiling tiles (or even missing ceiling tiles)? Do you see any signs of mold, dust, or cracks in the ceiling?

#8: Restrooms

Go into each restroom and check for functioning toilets and urinals. Make sure each sink works properly and is in good condition. Does each stall door close completely? Are the mirrors clean and in good condition? Do you have a sufficient number of trash receptacles in each restroom? Is each restroom adequately stocked with toilet paper, paper towels, hand soap, and the like?

#9: Drinking Fountains

Make sure each drinking fountain works properly and is in good condition.

#10: Kitchen

Carefully inspect the kitchen. Are there any expired food items in the pantry or refrigerator? Does the vent hood function correctly? Check the stove, microwave, sink, garbage disposal, and any floor drainage. Is the backsplash in good condition and clean? If the local health inspector arrived right now for a surprise inspection, would it pass?

#11: Lighting

Do all lights function properly? Do you need to replace any light bulbs or fixture coverings? Have lighting fixtures been dusted recently? Do all exit signs work? Do emergency lights function? Is the electrical panel properly labeled and accessible? Check extension cords and power strips to ensure none are overloaded.

#12: Fire Equipment

Do all smoke detectors function? Is the fire sprinkler system working correctly? Do you have the needed type of fire extinguishers in the right places? Have all fire extinguishers been inspected within the last month? Check the fire alarm panel/system to make sure it's in good condition.

#13: Baptistry

Make sure the baptistry is in good condition, no leaks, etc.

#14: Vents

Check all air vents. Make sure they are clear for proper airflow and free of dust/debris.

Since every church facility varies, this isn't an exhaustive list. However, this should give you an excellent start to your facility assessment. As you go through each area, make a note of any issues you find or repairs to make.

Many items may require a quick cleaning or repair to rectify. However, you will likely have a few items to put on your deferred maintenance list. Once you have a full list of items to fix, clean, or replace, prioritize any issues that impact safety and handle those immediately. From there, work your way down the list. Repeat this facility assessment at least annually, if not quarterly.

For a facility assessment checklist, go to:

http://www.smartchurchsolutions.com/entrustedresources.

THE CHOICE IS YOURS

Reading a book is easy. Taking action on what you learned from the text is a whole different story. However, reading the book is of no value if you don't do something with the knowledge you've gained. My prayer is that you're convinced, as I am, that you have a solemn duty to steward the facilities God has entrusted to your congregation carefully. Stewarding church facilities involves a great deal of non-ministry like tasks such as coordinating custodial teams, planning preventative maintenance, and setting money aside for retiring assets. While these activities don't *feel* like ministry, they support the ministry efforts of the church and help make ministry happen. Please take this charge seriously and invest the time, energy, and finances into doing this work with excellence.

Our team at Smart Church Solutions is always happy to support you in your efforts. We have tools, resources, and services that can make this process easier for you and your team. Please don't hesitate to reach out as you have questions. We also have several templates, checklists, and additional free resources available at:

http://www.smartchurchsolutions.com/entrustedresources.

ABOUT THE AUTHOR

Tim Cool is the founder of Smart Church Solutions and has assisted nearly 1,000 churches, (equating to over 5 million square feet) throughout the United States with their facility needs. He has collaborated with churches in the areas of facility needs analysis, design coordination, pre-construction and construction management as well as life cycle planning/facility management. Smart Church Solutions is also the developer of **eSPACE** software products including, Event Management, Work Order Management, Life Cycle Calculator, and IoT Integrations.

Tim is also the author of several books including, *Plan 4 It: The Essential Master Plans for Every Church, Successful Master Planning: More Than Pretty Pictures, Why Church Buildings Matter: The Story Of Your Space,* and *Church Locality,* co-authored with Jim Tomberlin.

Tim lives in Charlotte, North Carolina, with his wife of 35 years, Lisa, and is the proud father of his triplets who have left the nest.

NOTES

Introduction

1. https://www.dictionary.com/browse/steward

Section 1: The Case for Facility Stewardship

1. https://www.dictionary.com/browse/facility?s=t

2. https://www.dictionary.com/browse/stewardship?s=t

3. https://archive.epa.gov/stewardship/web/html/

Chapter 1: Fix It Now or Fix It Later (but at a higher price)

1. https://www.merriam-webster.com/dictionary/maintenance?utm_campaign=sd&utm_medium=serp&utm_source=jsonld

2. https://en.wikipedia.org/wiki/Deferred_maintenance

3. https://www.public.navy.mil/surfor/swmag/pages/the-test-of-time.aspx

4. Asset Lifecycle Model for Total Cost of Ownership Management, https://www.ifma.org/docs/default-source/knowledge-base/asset_lifecyle_model.pdf

Chapter 3: The Real Cost of Ownership

1. David S. Haviland, Life Cycle Cost Analysis 2: Using It In Practice (United States: American Institute of Architects, 1978)

Chapter 4: Energy Savings Equals Good Stewardship

1. Robert "Buck" Sheppard, "Clean HVAC System Coils Save Energy", Buildings.com, April 1, 2009, https://www.buildings.com/article-details/articleid/8282/title/clean-hvac-system-coils-save-energy

Chapter 5: First Impressions...Only One Shot

1. Mark Waltz, First Impressions (United States: Group Publishing, 2004)

Chapter 7: Deferred Maintenance (AKA...What we put off for later...)

1. Kevin Folsom, "Sustainable facilities vs. Sustainable Facilities", Facilities Manager, May/June 2008, https://files.eric.ed.gov/fulltext/EJ938799.pdf

Chapter 8: Utilities: Keeping the Lights On...But Not All the Time

1. Energystar, "Energy Efficiency Program Sponsor Frequently Asked Questions About ENERGY STAR Smart Thermostats", https://www.energystar.gov/products/heating_cooling/smart_thermostats/smart_thermostat_faq

2. https://ofmpub.epa.gov/sor_internet/registry/termreg/searchandretrieve/glossariesandkeywordlists/search.do;jsessionid=I4TgguK_HH6MN3D_mNw7klrFocrupy-UoBX5Rt7EzP1jjzvKOecz!-1968498344?details=&vocabName=Greening%20EPA%20Glossary&filterTerm=building%20automation%20system&checkedAcronym=false&checkedTerm=false&hasDefinitions=false&filterTerm=building%20automation%20system&filterMatchCriteria=Contains

3. "EPA study shows occupancy sensors reduce energy waste, demand", EC&M, December 3, 2001, https://www.ecmweb.com/construction/article/20893017/epa-study-shows-occupancy-sensors-reduce-energy-waste-demand

Chapter 9: Custodial: Cleanliness is Next to Godliness

1.   EPA, "Controlling Pollutants and Sources: Indoor Air Quality Design Tools for Schools", https://www.epa.gov/iaq-schools/controlling-pollutants-and-sources-indoor-air-quality-design-tools-schools

2.   "Getting A Grip On Floor Maintenance Costs And Safety Risks", Facility Executive, June 11, 2019, https://facilityexecutive.com/2019/06/entrance-mat-getting-grip-floor-maintenance-costs-safety-risks/

3.   https://www.goodreads.com/quotes/387614-we-don-t-rise-to-the-level-of-our-expectations-we

Chapter 10: Safety Isn't Overrated

1.   https://www.osha.gov/aboutosha

2.   https://www.osha.gov/top10citedstandards

3.   Andy Stanley, *Deep & Wide: Creating Churches Unchurched People Love to Attend* (United States: Zondervan, September 25, 2012)

Chapter 11: A Measured Approach to Church Security

1.   https://www.dhs.gov/see-something-say-something

Chapter 12: The Role of a Facility Manager

1.   Michel Theriault, Managing Facilities & Real Estate (United States: WoodStone Press, 2010)

Chapter 15: Facility Management Software

1.   https://www.goodreads.com/quotes/460142-if-you-fail-to-plan-you-are-planning-to-fail

Chapter 16: Budgeting

1. https://mungerconstruction.com/posts/value-your-building-by-maintaining-its-top-notch-condition/

2. http://www.geaslin.com/invers-square_rule.htm

3. https://dictionary.cambridge.org/us/dictionary/english/capital-reserve

Chapter 17: Facility Retirement Planning

1. https://churchexecutive.com/archives/what%E2%80%99s-the-real-cost-of-ownership

2. David S. Haviland, Life Cycle Cost Analysis 2: Using It In Practice (United States: American Institute of Architects, 1978)

3. Asset Lifecycle Model for Total Cost of Ownership Management, https://www.ifma.org/docs/default-source/knowledge-base/asset_lifecycle_model.pdf

Made in the USA
Monee, IL
01 March 2024

54251623R00085